Christianity's Sideshow

by RONALD JON SACHS I

Christianity's Sideshow

ISBN: 978-1-61170-293-4

Published by:

 **Robertson Publishing**™
www.RobertsonPublishing.com

Printed in the USA and UK on acid-free paper.

Front and back cover photos by Ronald J. Sachs

Dr. Robert Knapp has granted permission to include his article "How Magic & Miracles Spread Christianity", published in the January/February 2020 issue of *Biblical Archaeology Review*.

....

Major Contributors
Dr. Robert Knapp
Darrin Kissinger

Contributors
Dohn Kissinger
Richard Goyette
Doris Sachs

TABLE OF CONTENTS

Introduction

"CHRISTIANITY'S" SIDESHOW

The view from outside the Sideshow tent allowed a great
amount of diversity and separation regarding the question of
who are "Christians" and who are not "Christians."

Has the time come for us to rethink our priorities
with regard to our commitment to our God? To the teachings of
Jesus of Nazareth, OR to the tapestry, pageantry,
and magic of a "religion?"

"So many charismatic churches think they will grow if there are
enough miracles, but that really requires a basic discipleship
on a pathway for new believers because otherwise, they
freak out and leave."

About the Author

Ronald Jon Sachs I
Practical Theologian

Ron Sachs was born in 1934 in Pittsburgh, Pennsylvania. His father was employed by the federal government soon after Ron came along and was moved to new assignments about every 2-3 years. Thus, Ron grew up being the "odd person out." Ron was the new kid on the block, the new kid at school; the one who learned to be the "outsider." As Ron grew older, he found himself living and going to school in Europe in his "formative years," 14 to 18. He found himself most comfortable with the "street people." The "free style," the "con," the "right now," the questions, the "loneliness" and filling that time, became his personality and his comfort zone.

Ron served an apprenticeship as a conservator of works of art. Ron achieved much success and recognition in the fields of conservation, conserving works of art in and around Washington, D.C. for private as well as national treasures.

From working with historical objects, Ron became interested in the Bible as a book and how it became what it has become. His introduction to Codex Sinaiticus and its translation furthered his interest. Ron took on the task of personally translating portions of the Greek manuscripts of the Codex Sinaiticus. Ron began to question perceptions, manuscripts, myths, and the huge misuse of what the Bible says. Ron was influenced by William Ellery Channing (1780-1842) and John Wesley (1703-1791) eventually expanding his Unitarian theology in the United States. Ron has conducted classes and year-long discussions regarding the Bible within the United Methodist Church and is influenced by Bart D. Ehrman, John Dominic Crossan, Marcus Borg, and encouraged by persons who are not sure what is to be believed. Ron was ordained as a Unitarian minister over 50 years ago. Ron is a certified Conference Lay Minister within the United Methodist Church and has conducted classes/gatherings on "Christian" theology for 25+ years.

HOW
Magic & Miracles
Spread Christianity

"WITH THIS, YOU WILL CONQUER." The emperor Constantine took note, defeated his enemy Licinius, established Christianity as the focal religion of the Roman Empire, and changed history All very spectacular! It is also very misleading. It wasn't emperors who made Christianity It was ordinary men and women. It wasn't governors and generals who opposed Christianity; it was ordinary men and women. The story of ordinary people—their engagement with the supernatural through magic and miracles— makes sense of the origins of Christianity.

In the ancient world, the cares and concerns of such people are mundane: How will I survive? Can I do more—can I flourish? The hazards of life, illness, accident, personal confrontations—is it possible to control these? My family, my ancestors, my offspring— how can I honor, protect, and strengthen them? The responses to these questions rested on the belief in supernatural powers of all sorts surrounding and penetrating every aspect of life. There was no meaning, no problem solving, no hope, no society, unless these powers were recognized, mollified, and persuaded to do good— or at least to do no harm. Facing the new religion of Christianity, a polytheist's world of many powers suddenly collapsed into a world of one almighty, and mightily jealous, God, capable of great good and great harm. This was a literally tectonic reordering of the polytheist's bedrock beliefs. For some Jews, a fulfillment of Yahweh's plan through a messiah meant the collapse of a world based on Moses's Law—and the Temple priests and sacrifices— and its replacement by a self-reliant network of associations preparing for the end of the world.

Why would any ordinary polytheist or Jew voluntarily dispense with the received way of that banded together to pool their resources and maximize production and yield. As they grew and expanded, so did their site, which eventually grew to house a cult place, constructed and established as a monumental temple. The erection of the temple is a hefty undertaking that necessitated administrative organization and exhibited a high level of craftsmanship and knowledge of ancient Near Eastern conventions. The construction of the Tel Moza temple should be viewed as a reflection of the complexity of the local community and an indication of a level of civic administrative formation by the early ninth century B.C.E. in this region — perhaps even an autonomous Moza polity.

Who *exactly* constructed the temple in the early ninth century B.C.E.? And were these people associated with the rise of Jerusalem and the emergence of the Kingdom of Judah? And how did this temple operate successfully in the shadow of the Jerusalem Temple throughout its entire lifespan, especially when the Bible makes no mention of any such temple and, moreover, says all other shrines were destroyed? All we know so far is that when it was constructed, The Moza temple was likely the undertaking of a local group, but by the Iron HE period, it was clearly under Judahite rule and must therefore have been royally sanctioned by the realm. The rest remains to be discovered.

By about AD. 150, four generations after the crucifixion, all eyewitnesses (ordinary folk) were dead. The new Jesus-sect (also called the Way) had begun to be interpreted, spread, and controlled by an elite within the movement. These men, closely tied intellectually and culturally to the polytheist culture around them, were mostly concerned with touting Christianity using categories of thought and action familiar to educated Romans and Greeks. This "orthodox" (literally, "straight-thinking"), elite-conceived picture elided ordinary men and women in important ways. Retrieving the early Christians and Christianity largely unseen by the orthodox version of the beginnings — essentially writing about "invisible Christians" — is hard because ordinary people are usually voiceless in the material that survives from antiquity. It is doubly hard because discussion of early Christianity is usually written in the almost indelible ink of elite discourse — both ancient and modern. But by critically using Latin and Greek literary materials, Jewish sources, the New Testament writings of the early church, and comparative studies of non-ancient societies, it is possible to unveil those near invisible souls, both polytheist and Jewish, and to understand how they interacted in a world noncompliance, others threatening violence if the society-upending preaching did not stop. Early Christians had to convince polytheists that *Jesus* was worth the risk of change. These two threads, Jewish traditions and polytheist culture, become interwoven as Christianity moved outward from its homeland, Judea, into the Roman Empire. On the one hand, this Jesussect met with strong resistance, not so much from the Roman government, but from ordinary Jews and polytheists whose lives were being disrupted—a resistance that led to bloodshed on numerous occasions. Yet some polytheists embraced the new sect. Such conversions did not come about on the basis of Christianity's supposedly superior morality or philosophical treatments of life's issues. Rather, people changed because of magic and miracles—because these were the central and virtually only mechanism for convincing ordinary people to give up their ancestral relationships to supernatural powers. In demonstrating the ability to direct supernatural power, Jesus and the early Christian apostles met polytheism on its own ground by focusing on the ability to help people deal with life's contingencies and boasted that their Way showed itself superior. Jews, too, believed in miracles. They also could be convinced of the new sect's legitimacy because miracles were a long-accepted proof of Yahweh's power. To the elite, who gradually gained control of orthodoxy, miracles were an embarrassment, evidence of everyday religiosity that circumvented their favorite method of discourse—increasingly erudite, abstract, and pagan-influenced explanations of the meaning of the crucifixion and resurrection. But for ordinary people, "show me the miracle" was the litmus test of supernatural power. Enthusiastic Christians rose to the challenge in wide-ranging and imaginative ways—and thereby won over Jews and polytheists alike.

By the end of the third century Christianity had become a movement with an organizational structure, theology, and popular appeal. Perhaps as many as 10 percent of urban dwellers and 3 percent of rural inhabitants believed in some form of Christianity. In all likelihood, the movement would have continued as one option among many in the polytheist world—no better, no worse than others— appealing to a few, but hardly to all. Constantine's cross in the sky canceled that trajectory Instead, Christianity became an imperial religion. Its appeal and spread no longer depended on meeting people's needs through demonstrations of power. Top-down replaced bottom-up. Hand in hand with empire, it began its march through history Christ's triumphant return and the vengeful end of time always receding before it.

Supernatural power remained at the center, but now in the service of a much grander movement than Jesus of Nazareth could ever have imaged in the dust and heat of far-off Judea — as magic and miracles proved his authority.

~ ~ ~ ~ ~

Robert Knapp's article *How Magic & Miracles Spread Christianity* was published in Biblical Archaeology Review. BAR, Jan/Feb 2020, pp. 50-53.

Robert Knapp is Professor Emeritus in the Classics at UC Berkeley and has also authored **The Dawn of Christianity. People and Gods in a Time of Magic and Miracles.**

Are there too many unbelievable, misinterpreted, downright falsehoods, in the Bible we have sitting on our coffee table that we don't understand?

About that virgin birth for example. Luke 1:25. This translates to, "maid or maiden." In the Jewish Isaiah 7:14 the word translates to "girl of 13 to 16." And not the word virgin as used today. Also translations in our Bibles show a bias, such as in Romans 16:7. Junianus, Junia, is a name for women. These were changed to Junias, Junianus, a man's name in the King James version of the Bible and the American Standard Bible. And Matthew 24:36 ….Not even the angles of heaven, <u>neither the Son,</u> but the Father only." <u>Neither the Son</u> was removed because they suggested that Jesus was not equal to God. Modern translations put that back into Bibles.

Paul, was first one to write about Jesus.

We should keep in mind that Paul's letters to his established churches were the very first writings produced regarding Jesus. Paul does not quote Jesus anywhere in the New testament. Paul was a Pharisaic Jew, educated as a Jewish Pharisee as well as in the Greek language and customs. These letters were written around 50-70 C.E. About 20-50 years after the Crucifixion of Jesus. Paul never heard Jesus speak. The letters were all about the problems that the churches that Paul started were having; problems within their congregations. The same kind of problems we have in the congregations that we have today; plus, in the case of the Corinth church, the pagan temple that dominated the town offering prostitution on a large scale. Paul's reference to "Chloe's people" (a female name) was giving Paul the lowdown on what was astray. Unfortunately, none of the original letters survived in the original text. As they were passed around and re-copied again and again none of these written in the first century survived the centuries. Then to complicate the matter, other "letters" ascribed to Paul were produced in his name; such as 1st & 2nd Timothy and Titus. Then, also debated are Colossians, Ephesian and 2nd Thessalonians. These scriptures wander off the path that Paul or Jesus expounded in their teachings. And sometimes counter what

Jesus taught. About 50% of the New Testament is attributed to Paul. This was the start of "Christianity, "not the Bible of 367 CE.

And do we read what Jesus taught? When was he born? The "Scriptures" say he was born during the reign of King Herod 47-4 BC. So, Jesus was born around 4 BC, baptized at 30 and died at the age of 33. There is convincing historical evidence that a wise man who taught what we perceive to be Jesus' wisdom indeed did live at that time.

Some of the Bible stories are hard to believe. Nazareth is about 98 miles from Bethlehem on today's roads and highways. Roads of the first century? A pregnant woman and man walking about 20 to 25 miles a day would take an unbelievable length of time to make the trip. Is the Bethlehem story in our Bible fabricated to fulfill an old Jewish prophecy? Again, in our Bible we have the "virgin" story and the problem of translation from Aramaic, spoken by Jesus, into Greek, then to English. When the Hebrew was translated to the Greek in the Septuagint regarding the virgin issue, it was translated as ΠΑΡΘCΝOC. This is the same as rendered in Matthew 1:23 and Luke 1:25. This translates to, "maid or maiden." In the Jewish Isaiah 7:14 the word, translates to "girl of 13 to 16." And not today's meaning of virgin.

Apollonius of Tyana was living at the same time as Jesus with the same messages and preforming healings same as attributed to Jesus of Nazareth. However, Apollonius was Greek and was written about by the Greeks, in Greece. In Greece he is call a philosopher. The Greek writers recording Jesus develop Jesus of Nazareth as a divine person connected to the Jewish faith. Is this a possible connection?

We must keep in mind that before Orthodox Christianity was organized, there were numerous groups that worshiped Jesus of Nazareth.

Carpocratians had a reputation for being a rowdy group with pageantry and the sharing of everything a person owned—including wives.

Docetism was the belief that Jesus could not have been human, therefore, could not have suffered on the cross.

Ebonite was a Jewish sect that Peter and James, the brother of Jesus followed and they remained Jews. They believed that Jesus was fully human. They lasted about 1000 years before fading away.

Gnostics were a loose group of different theologies that were not "Orthodox." They had secret knowledge. They also became a "catch all" for theologians who saw them "different" from "Orthodox Theology."

Marcionites taught Paul's teachings. Some thought them "anti-Jewish."

Theodotianms, maintained that Jesus was just a man of normal birth, but chosen by God at His baptism to be the savior of the world. They were popular with the Romans.

There were at least 10 different theologies with doctrines and many followers before "Orthodoxy" prevailed.

So, is it possible that historical records have muddied the New Testament biblical story? The Bible, as we know it today, was written long after Jesus was crucified, by persons who never heard Jesus speak. And as Luke states "Since many have undertaken this set down and orderly account of the events that have been fulfilled among us just as they were handed on to us by those who from the beginning where eyewitnesses and servants of the word." All are hearsay or oral tradition.

Then, Athanasius, Bishop of Alexandria, after his list of the Old Testament books, (Not the same as the Jewish Scriptures), he listed the 27 books of the New Testament in 367 CA, and also announced the date for Easter. Even when the New Testament disagrees when Jesus was crucified. Before or after the Passover. This all 300 years after Jesus' crucifixion. Then Athanasius ordered all the other Scriptures, Gospels, writings about Jesus destroyed. Fortunately, some disobeyed. These records and historical documents have been rediscovered.

Outside the Sideshow Tent
All is Glitter, Magic, Miracles, Spectacle
But Found Inside the Sideshow Tent?

Do many "Christians" ever go inside the tent?

Behind the Magic and Miracles? Do they really know about Y'shua Ben Y'hosep, Y'shua of Nazareth and who the Greek writers of the New Testament named, Jesus of Nazareth?

....

In 1813 Thomas Jefferson wrote a letter to his friend and confidant, John Adams in reference to the Bible. *"We must reduce our volume to the simple evangelist, select, even from them, the very words only of Jesus. There will be remaining the most sublime and benevolent code of morals which has ever been offered to man."*

The following is an adaptation of Thomas Jefferson's book, removing the "magic" and "miracles" attributed to Jesus, and leaving His wisdom and teachings, reproduced in a modern English language, as opposed to Jefferson's translations from Greek, French, and Latin into English.

The Life And Morals Of Jesus Of Nazareth

(**Mat**-Matthew, **Mar**-Mark. **Lu**-Luke, **Jo**-John.
(These are the references to be found in your Bible.)

Lu 2:1-7 - In those days a decree went out from Caesar Augustus that all the world should be enrolled (Taxed). This was the first enrollment, when Quirin'i-us was governor of Syria. And all went to be enrolled, each to his own city. And Joseph also went up from Galilee, from the city of Nazareth, to Judea, to the city of David, which is called Bethlehem, because he was of the house and lineage of David, to be enrolled (taxed) with Mary, his betrothed, who was with child. And while they were there, the time came for her to be delivered. And she gave birth to her first-born son and wrapped him in swaddling clothes, and laid him in a manger, because there was no place for them in the inn.

Lu 2:21 - And at the end of eight days, when he was circumcised, he was called Jesus, the name given by the angel before he was conceived in the womb.

Lu 2:39-40 - And when they had performed everything according to the law of the Lord, they returned into Galilee, to their own city, Nazareth. And the child grew and became strong, filled with wisdom; and the favor of God was upon him.

Lu 2:42-45 - And when he was twelve years old, they went up to Jerusalem according to custom; and when the feast was ended, as they were returning, the boy Jesus stayed behind in Jerusalem. His parents did not know it, but supposing him to be in the company of their kinfolk and acquaintances, they went a day's journey, and they sought him among their kinsfolk and acquaintances; and when they did not find him, they returned to Jerusalem, seeking him.

Lu 2:46-48 - After three days they found him in the temple, sitting among the teachers, listening to them and asking them questions; and all who heard him were amazed at his understanding and his answers. And when they saw him they were astonished; and his mother said to him, "Son, why have you treated us so? Behold, your father and I have been looking for you anxiously."

Lu 2:51-52 - And he went down with them and came to Nazareth, and was obedient to them; and his mother kept all these things in her heart. And Jesus increased in wisdom and in stature, and in favor with God and man.

Lu 3:1-2 - In the fifteenth year of the reign of Tiber'i-us Caesar, Pontius Pilate being governor of Judea, and Herod being tetrarch of Galilee, and his brother Philip tetrarch of the region of Iturae'a and Trachoni'tis, and Lysa'ni-as tetrarch of Abile'ne, in the high-priesthood of Annas and Ca'iaphas, the word of God came to John the son of Zechari'ah in the wilderness;

Mar 1:4 - John the baptizer appeared in the wilderness, preaching a baptism of repentance for the forgiveness of sins.

Mat 3:4-6 - Now John wore a garment of camel's hair, and a leather girdle around his waist; and his food was locusts and wild honey. Then went out to him Jerusalem and all Judea and all the region about the Jordan, and they were baptized by him in the river Jordan, confessing their sins.

Mat 3:13 - Then Jesus came from Galilee to the Jordan to John, to be baptized by him.

Lu 3:23 - Jesus, when he began his ministry, was about thirty years of age, being the son (as was supposed) of Joseph, the son of Heli,

Jo 2:12 - After this he went down to Caper'na-um, with his mother and his brothers and his disciples; and there they stayed for a few days.

Jo 2:13-16 - The Passover of the Jews was at hand, and Jesus went up to Jerusalem. In the temple he found those who were selling oxen and sheep and pigeons, and the money-changers at their business. And making a whip of cords, he drove them all, with the sheep and oxen, out of the temple; and he poured out the coins of the money-changers and overturned their tables. And he told those who sold the pigeons, "Take these things away; you shall not make my Father's house a house of trade."

Jo 3:22 - After this Jesus and his disciples went into the land of Judea; there he remained with them and baptized.

Mat 4:12 - Now when he heard that John had been arrested, he withdrew into Galilee;

Mar 6:17-23 - For Herod had sent and seized John, and bound him in prison for the sake of Hero'di-as, his brother Philip's wife; because he had married her. For John said to Herod, "It is not lawful for you to have your brother's wife." And Hero'di-as had a grudge against him, and wanted to kill him. But she could not, for Herod feared John, knowing that he was a righteous and holy man, and kept him safe. When he heard him, he was much perplexed; and yet he heard him gladly. But an opportunity came when Herod on his birthday gave a banquet for his courtiers and officers and the leading men of Galilee. For when Hero'di-as' daughter came in and danced, she pleased Herod and his guests; and the king said to the girl, "Ask me for whatever you wish, and I will grant it." And he vowed to her, "Whatever you ask me, I will give you, even half of my kingdom."

Mar 6:24-28 - And she went out, and said to her mother, "What shall I ask?" And she said, "The head of John the baptizer." And she came in immediately with haste to the king, and asked, saying, "I want you to give me at once the head of John the Baptist on a platter." And the king was exceedingly sorry; but because of his oaths and his guests he did not want to break his word to her. And immediately the king sent a soldier of the guard and gave orders to bring his head. He went and beheaded him in the prison, and brought his head on a platter, and gave it to the girl; and the girl gave it to her mother.

Mar 1:21-22 - And they went into Caper'na-um; and immediately on the sabbath he entered the synagogue and taught. And they were astonished at his teaching, for he taught them as one who had authority, and not as the scribes.

Mat 12:1-5 - At that time Jesus went through the grain fields on the sabbath; his disciples were hungry, and they began to pluck heads of grain and to eat. But when the Pharisees saw it, they said to him, "Look, your disciples are doing what is not lawful to do on the sabbath." He said to them, "Have you not read what David did, when he was hungry, and those who were with him: how he entered the house of God and ate the bread of the Presence, which it was not lawful for him to eat nor for those who were with him, but only for the priests? Or have you not read in the law how on the sabbath the priests in the temple profane the sabbath, and are guiltless?

Mar 6:24-28 - And she went out, and said to her mother," what shall I ask?" And she said," the head of John the baptizer." And she came in immediately with a haste to the king, and asked, saying," I want you to give me at once the head of John the Baptist on a platter." And the king was exceedingly sorry; but because of his oaths and his guests he did not one to break his word to her. And immediately the king sent a soldier of the guard and gave orders to bring his head. He went and beheaded him in prison, and brought his head on a platter, and gave it to the girl; and the girl gave it to her mother.

Mar 1:21-22 - And they went into Caper'na-um; and immediately on the sabbath he entered the synagogue and taught. And they were astonished at his teaching, for he taught them as one who had authority, and not as the scribes.

Mat 12:1-5 - At that time Jesus went through the grain fields on the sabbath; his disciples were hungry, and they began to pluck heads of grain and to eat. But when the Pharisees saw it, they said to him, "Look, your disciples are doing what is not lawful to do on the sabbath." He said to them, "Have you not read what David did, when he was hungry, and those who were with him: how he entered the house of God and ate the bread of the Presence, which it was not lawful for him to eat nor for those who were with him, but only for the priests? Or have you not read in the law how on the sabbath the priests in the temple profane the sabbath, and are guiltless?

Mat 5:1-12 - Seeing the crowds, he went up on the mountain, and when he sat down his disciples came to him. And he opened his mouth and taught them, saying: "Blessed are the poor in spirit, for theirs is the kingdom of heaven. "Blessed are those who mourn, for they shall be comforted. "Blessed are the meek, for they shall inherit the earth. "Blessed are those who hunger and thirst for righteousness, for they shall be satisfied. "Blessed are the merciful, for they shall obtain mercy. "Blessed are the pure in heart, for they shall see God. "Blessed are the peacemakers, for they shall be called sons of God. "Blessed are those who are persecuted for righteousness' sake, for theirs is the kingdom of heaven. "Blessed are you when men revile you and persecute you and utter all kinds of evil against you falsely on my account. Rejoice and be glad, for your reward is great in heaven, for so men persecuted the prophets who were before you.

Lu 6:24-26 - "But woe to you that are rich, for you have received your consolation. "Woe to you that are full now, for you shall hunger. "Woe to you that laugh now, for you shall mourn and weep. "Woe to you, when all men speak well of you, for so their fathers did to the false prophets.

Mat 5:13-14 - "You are the salt of the earth; but if salt has lost its taste, how shall its saltness be restored? It is no longer good for anything except to be thrown out and trodden under foot by men. "You are the light of the world. A city set on a hill cannot be hid.

Mat 5:15-24 - Nor do men light a lamp and put it under a bushel, but on a stand, and it gives light to all in the house. Let your light so shine before men, that they may see your good works and give glory to your Father who is in heaven. "Think not that I have come to abolish the law and the prophets; I have come not to abolish them but to fulfil them. For truly, I say to you, till heaven and earth pass away, not an iota, not a dot, will pass from the law until all is accomplished. Whoever then relaxes one of the least of these commandments and teaches men so, shall be called least in the kingdom of heaven; but he who does them and teaches them shall be called great in the kingdom of heaven. For I tell you, unless your righteousness exceeds that of the scribes and Pharisees, you will never enter the kingdom of heaven. "You have heard that it was said to the men of old, 'You shall not kill; and whoever kills shall be liable to judgment.' But I say to you that everyone who is angry with his brother shall be liable to judgment; whoever insults his brother shall be liable to the council, and whoever says, 'You fool!' shall be liable to the hell of fire. So if you are offering your gift at the altar, and there remember that your brother has something against you, leave your gift there before the altar and go; first be reconciled to your brother, and then come and offer your gift.

Mat 5:25-35 - Make friends quickly with your accuser, while you are going with him to court, lest your accuser hand you over to the judge, and the judge to the guard, and you be put in prison; truly, I say to you, you will never get out till you have paid the last penny. "You have heard that it was said, 'You shall not commit adultery.' But I say to you that everyone who looks at a woman lustfully has already committed adultery with her in his heart. If your right eye causes you to sin, pluck it out and throw it away; it is better that you lose one of your members than that your whole body be thrown into hell. And if your right hand causes you to sin, cut it off and throw it away; it is better that you lose one of your members than that your whole body go into hell. "It was also said, 'Whoever divorces his wife, let him give her a certificate of divorce.' But I say to you that everyone who divorces his wife, except on the ground of unchastity, makes her an adulteress; and whoever marries a divorced woman commits adultery. "Again, you have heard that it was said to the men of old, 'You shall not swear falsely, but shall perform to the Lord what you have sworn.' But I say to you, Do not swear at all, either by heaven, for it is the throne of God, or by the earth, for it is his footstool, or by Jerusalem, for it is the city of the great King.

Mat 5:36-47 - And do not swear by your head, for you cannot make one hair white or black. Let what you say be simply 'Yes' or 'No'; anything more than this comes from evil. "You have heard that it was said, 'An eye for an eye and a tooth for a tooth.' But I say to you, "Do not resist one who is evil. But if any one strikes you on the right cheek, turn to him the other also; and if anyone would sue you and take your coat, let him have your cloak as well; and if any one forces you to go one mile, go with him two miles. Give to him who begs from you, and do not refuse him who would borrow from you. "You have heard that it was said, 'You shall love your neighbor and hate your enemy.' But I say to you, Love your enemies and pray for those who persecute you, so that you may be sons of your Father who is in heaven; for he makes his sun rise on the evil and on the good, and sends rain on the just and on the unjust. For if you love those who love you, what reward have you? Do not even the tax collectors do the same? And if you salute only your brethren, what more are you doing than others? Do not even the Gentiles do the same?

Lu 6:34-36 - And if you lend to those from whom you hope to receive, what credit is that to you? Even sinners lend to sinners, to receive as much again. But love your enemies, and do good, and lend, expecting nothing in return; and your reward will be great, and you will be sons of the Most High; for he is kind to the ungrateful and the selfish. Be merciful, even as your Father is merciful.

Mat 6:1-8 - "Beware of practicing your piety before men in order to be seen by them; for then you will have no reward from your Father who is in heaven. "Thus, when you give alms, sound no trumpet before you, as the hypocrites do in the synagogues and in the streets, that they may be praised by men. Truly, I say to you, they have received their reward. But when you give alms, do not let your left hand know what your right hand is doing, so that your alms may be in secret; and your Father who sees in secret will reward you. "And when you pray, you must not be like the hypocrites; for they love to stand and pray in the synagogues and at the street corners, that they may be seen by men. Truly, I say to you, they have received their reward. But when you pray, go into your room and shut the door and pray to your Father who is in secret; and your Father who sees in secret will reward you. "And in praying do not heap up empty phrases as the Gentiles do; for they think that they will be heard for their many words. Do not be like them, for your Father knows what you need before you ask him.

Mat 6:9-22 - Pray then like this: Our Father who art in heaven, Hallowed be thy name. Thy kingdom comes. Thy will be done, On earth as it is in heaven. Give us this day our daily bread; And forgive us our debts, As we also have forgiven our debtors; And lead us not into temptation, But deliver us from evil. For if you forgive men their trespasses, your heavenly Father also will forgive you; but if you do not forgive men their trespasses, neither will your Father forgive your trespasses. "And when you fast, do not look dismal, like the hypocrites, for they disfigure their faces that their fasting may be seen by men. Truly, I say to you, they have received their reward. But when you fast, anoint your head and wash your face, that your fasting may not be seen by men but by your Father who is in secret; and your Father who sees in secret will reward you. "Do not lay up for yourselves treasures on earth, where moth and rust consume and where thieves break in and steal, but lay up for yourselves treasures in heaven, where neither moth nor rust consumes and where thieves do not break in and steal. For where your treasure is, there will your heart be also. "The eye is the lamp of the body. So, if your eye is sound, your whole body will be full of light;

Mat 6:23-34 - but if your eye is not sound, your whole body will be full of darkness. If then the light in you is darkness, how great is the darkness! "No one can serve two masters; for either he will hate the one and love the other, or he will be devoted to the one and despise the other. You cannot serve God and mammon. "Therefore, I tell you, do not be anxious about your life, what you shall eat or what you shall drink, nor about your body, what you shall put on. Is not life more than food, and the body more than clothing? Look at the birds of the air: they neither sow nor reap nor gather into barns, and yet your heavenly Father feeds them. Are you not of more value than they? And which of you by being anxious can add one cubit to his span of life? And why are you anxious about clothing? Consider the lilies of the field, how they grow; they neither toil nor spin; yet I tell you, even Solomon in all his glory was not arrayed like one of these. But if God so clothes the grass of the field, which today is alive and tomorrow is thrown into the oven, will he not much more clothe you, O men of little faith? Therefore, do not be anxious, saying, 'What shall we eat?' or 'What shall we drink?' or 'What shall we wear?' For the Gentiles seek all these things; and your heavenly Father knows that you need them all. But seek first his kingdom and his righteousness, and all these things shall be yours as well. "Therefore, do not be anxious about tomorrow, for tomorrow will be anxious for itself. Let the day's own trouble be sufficient for the day.

Mat 7:1-2 - "Judge not, that you be not judged. For with the judgment you pronounce you will be judged, and the measure you give will be the measure you get.

Lu 6:38 - give, and it will be given to you; good measure, pressed down, shaken together, running over, will be put into your lap. For the measure you give will be the measure you get back."

Mat 7:3-12 - Why do you see the speck that is in your brother's eye, but do not notice the log that is in your own eye? Or how can you say to your brother, 'Let me take the speck out of your eye,' when there is the log in your own eye? You hypocrite, first take the log out of your own eye, and then you will see clearly to take the speck out of your brother's eye. "Do not give dogs what is holy; and do not throw your pearls before swine, lest they trample them under foot and turn to attack you. "Ask, and it will be given you; seek, and you will find; knock, and it will be opened to you. For every one who asks receives, and he who seeks finds, and to him who knocks it will be opened. Or what man of you, if his son asks him for bread, will give him a stone? Or if he asks for a fish, will give him a serpent? If you then, who are evil, know how to give good gifts to your children, how much more will your Father who is in heaven give good things to those who ask him! So whatever you wish that men would do to you, do so to them; for this is the law and the prophets.

Mat 7:13-20 - "Enter by the narrow gate; for the gate is wide and the way is easy, that leads to destruction, and those who enter by it are many. For the gate is narrow and the way is hard, that leads to life, and those who find it are few. "Beware of false prophets, who come to you in sheep's clothing but inwardly are ravenous wolves. You will know them by their fruits. Are grapes gathered from thorns, or figs from thistles? So, every sound tree bears good fruit, but the bad tree bears evil fruit. A sound tree cannot bear evil fruit, nor can a bad tree bear good fruit. Every tree that does not bear good fruit is cut down and thrown into the fire. Thus, you will know them by their fruits.

Mat 12:35-37 - The good man out of his good treasure brings forth good, and the evil man out of his evil treasure brings forth evil. I tell you, on the day of judgment men will render account for every careless word they utter; for by your words you will be justified, and by your words you will be condemned."

Mat 7:24-25 - "Everyone then who hears these words of mine and does them will be like a wise man who built his house upon the rock; and the rain fell, and the floods came, and the winds blew and beat upon that house, but it did not fall, because it had been founded on the rock.

Mat 7:26-29 - And everyone who hears these words of mine and does not do them will be like a foolish man who built his house upon the sand; and the rain fell, and the floods came, and the winds blew and beat against that house, and it fell; and great was the fall of it." And when Jesus finished these sayings, the crowds were astonished at his teaching, for he taught them as one who had authority, and not as their scribes.

Mat 8:1 - When he came down from the mountain, great crowds followed him;

Mar 6:6 - And he marveled because of their unbelief. And he went about among the villages teaching.

at 11:28-30 - Come to me, all who labor and are heavy laden, and I will give you rest. Take my yoke upon you, and learn from me; for I am gentle and lowly in heart, and you will find rest for your souls. For my yoke is easy, and my burden is light."

Lu 7:36-38 - One of the Pharisees asked him to eat with him, and he went into the Pharisee's house, and took his place at table. And behold, a woman of the city, who was a sinner, when she learned that he was at table in the Pharisee's house, brought an alabaster flask of ointment, and standing behind him at his feet, weeping, she began to wet his feet with her tears, and wiped them with the hair of her head, and kissed his feet, and anointed them with the ointment.

Lu 7:39-46 - Now when the Pharisee who had invited him saw it, he said to himself, "If this man were a prophet, he would have known who and what sort of woman this is who is touching him, for she is a sinner." And Jesus answering said to him, "Simon, I have something to say to you." And he answered, "What is it, Teacher?" "A certain creditor had two debtors; one owed five hundred denarii, and the other fifty. When they could not pay, he forgave them both. Now which of them will love him more?" Simon answered, "The one, I suppose, to whom he forgave more." And he said to him, "You have judged rightly." Then turning toward the woman, he said to Simon, "Do you see this woman? I entered your house, you gave me no water for my feet, but she has wet my feet with her tears and wiped them with her hair. You gave me no kiss, but from the time I came in she has not ceased to kiss my feet. You did not anoint my head with oil, but she has anointed my feet with ointment.

Mar 3:31-35 - And his mother and his brothers came; and standing outside they sent to him and called him. And a crowd was sitting about him; and they said to him, "Your mother and your brothers are outside, asking for you." And he replied, "Who are my mother and my brothers?" And looking around on those who sat about him, he said, "Here are my mother and my brothers! Whoever does the will of God is my brother, and sister, and mother."

Lu 12:1-7 - In the meantime, when so many thousands of the multitude had gathered together that they trod upon one another, he began to say to his disciples first, "Beware of the leaven of the Pharisees, which is hypocrisy. Nothing is covered up that will not be revealed, or hidden that will not be known. Therefore, whatever you have said in the dark shall be heard in the light, and what you have whispered in private rooms shall be proclaimed upon the housetops. "I tell you, my friends, do not fear those who kill the body, and after that have no more that they can do. But I will warn you whom to fear: fear him who, after he has killed, has power to cast into hell; yes, I tell you, fear him! Are not five sparrows sold for two pennies? And not one of them is forgotten before God. Why, even the hairs of your head are all numbered. Fear not; you are of more value than many sparrows.

Lu 12:13-16 - One of the multitudes said to him, "Teacher, bid my brother divide the inheritance with me." But he said to him, "Man, who made me a judge or divider over you?" And he said to them, "Take heed, and beware of all covetousness; for a man's life does not consist in the abundance of his possessions." And he told them a parable, saying, "The land of a rich man brought forth plentifully;

Lu 12:17-30 - and he thought to himself, 'What shall I do, for I have nowhere to store my crops?' And he said, 'I will do this: I will pull down my barns, and build larger ones; and there I will store all my grain and my goods. And I will say to my soul, Soul, you have ample goods laid up for many years; take your ease, eat, drink, be merry.' But God said to him, 'Fool! This night your soul is required of you; and the things you have prepared, whose will they be?' So is he who lays up treasure for himself, and is not rich toward God." And he said to his disciples, "Therefore I tell you, do not be anxious about your life, what you shall eat, nor about your body, what you shall put on. For life is more than food, and the body more than clothing. Consider the ravens: they neither sow nor reap, they have neither storehouse nor barn, and yet God feeds them. Of how much more value are you than the birds! And which of you by being anxious can add a cubit to his span of life? If then you are not able to do as small a thing as that, why are you anxious about the rest? Consider the lilies, how they grow; they neither toil nor spin; yet I tell you, even Solomon in all his glory was not arrayed like one of these. But if God so clothes the grass which is alive in the field today and tomorrow is thrown into the oven, how much more will he clothe you, O men of little faith! And do not seek what you are to eat and what you are to drink, nor be of anxious mind. For all the nations of the world seek these things; and your Father knows that you need them.

Lu 12:31-43 - Instead, seek his kingdom, and these things shall be yours as well. "Fear not, little flock, for it is your Father's good pleasure to give you the kingdom. Sell your possessions, and give alms; provide yourselves with purses that do not grow old, with a treasure in the heavens that does not fail, where no thief approaches and no moth destroy. For where your treasure is, there will your heart be also. "Let your loins be girded and your lamps burning, and be like men who are waiting for their master to come home from the marriage feast, so that they may open to him at once when he comes and knocks. Blessed are those servants whom the master finds awake when he comes; truly, I say to you, he will gird himself and have them sit at table, and he will come and serve them. If he comes in the second watch, or in the third, and finds them so, blessed are those servants! But know this, that if the householder had known at what hour the thief was coming, he would not have left his house to be broken into. You also must be ready; for the Son of man is coming at an unexpected hour." Peter said, "Lord, are you telling this parable for us or for all?" And the Lord said, "Who then is the faithful and wise steward, whom his master will set over his household, to give them their portion of food at the proper time? Blessed is that servant whom his master when he comes will find so doing.

Lu 12:44-48 - Truly, I say to you, he will set him over all his possessions. But if that servant says to himself, 'My master is delayed in coming,' and begins to beat the menservants and the maidservants, and to eat and drink and get drunk, the master of that servant will come on a day when he does not expect him and at an hour he does not know, and will punish him, and put him with the unfaithful. And that servant who knew his master's will, but did not make ready or act according to his will, shall receive a severe beating. But he who did not know, and did what deserved a beating, shall receive a light beating. Every one to whom much is given, of him will much be required; and of him to whom men commit much they will demand the more.

Lu 12:54-59 - He also said to the multitudes, "When you see a cloud rising in the west, you say at once, 'A shower is coming'; and so it happens. And when you see the south wind blowing, you say, 'There will be scorching heat'; and it happens. You hypocrites! You know how to interpret the appearance of earth and sky; but why do you not know how to interpret the present time? "And why do you not judge for yourselves what is right? As you go with your accuser before the magistrate, make an effort to settle with him on the way, lest he drag you to the judge, and the judge hand you over to the officer, and the officer put you in prison. I tell you; you will never get out till you have paid the very last copper."

Lu 13:1-9 - There were some present at that very time who told him of the Galileans whose blood Pilate had mingled with their sacrifices. And he answered them, "Do you think that these Galileans were worse sinners than all the other Galileans, because they suffered thus? I tell you, no; but unless you repent you will all likewise perish. Or those eighteen upon whom the tower in Silo'am fell and killed them, do you think that they were worse offenders than all the others who dwelt in Jerusalem? I tell you, No; but unless you repent you will all likewise perish." And he told this parable: "A man had a fig tree planted in his vineyard; and he came seeking fruit on it and found none. And he said to the vinedresser, 'Lo, these three years I have come seeking fruit on this fig tree, and I find none. Cut it down; why should it use up the ground?' And he answered him, 'Let it alone, sir, this year also, till I dig about it and put on manure. And if it bears fruit next year, well and good; but if not, you can cut it down.'"

Lu 11:37-41 - While he was speaking, a Pharisee asked him to dine with him; so he went in and sat at table. The Pharisee was astonished to see that he did not first wash before dinner. And the Lord said to him, "Now you Pharisees cleanse the outside of the cup and of the dish, but inside you are full of extortion and wickedness. You fools! Did not he who made the outside make the inside also? But give for alms those things which are within; and behold, everything is clean for you.

Lu 11:42-46 - "But woe to you Pharisees! for you tithe mint and rue and every herb, and neglect justice and the love of God; these you ought to have done, without neglecting the others. Woe to you Pharisees! for you love the best seat in the synagogues and salutations in the market places. Woe to you! for you are like graves which are not seen, and men walk over them without knowing it." One of the lawyers answered him, "Teacher, in saying this you reproach us also." And he said, "Woe to you lawyers also! for you load men with burdens hard to bear, and you yourselves do not touch the burdens with one of your fingers.

Lu 11:52-54 - Woe to you lawyers! for you have taken away the key of knowledge; you did not enter yourselves, and you hindered those who were entering." As he went away from there, the scribes and the Pharisees began to press him hard, and to provoke him to speak of many things, lying in wait for him, to catch at something he might say.

Mat 13:1-4 - That same day Jesus went out of the house and sat beside the sea. And great crowds gathered about him, so that he got into a boat and sat there; and the whole crowd stood on the beach. And he told them many things in parables, saying: "A sower went out to sow. And as he sowed, some seeds fell along the path, and the birds came and devoured them.

Mat 13:5-9 - Other seeds fell on rocky ground, where they had not much soil, and immediately they sprang up, since they had no depth of soil, but when the sun rose, they were scorched; and since they had no root they withered away. Other seeds fell upon thorns, and the thorns grew up and choked them. Other seeds fell on good soil and brought forth grain, some a hundredfold, some sixty, some thirty. He who has ears, let him hear."

Mar 4:10 - And when he was alone, those who were about him with the twelve asked him concerning the parables.

Mat 13:18-23 - "Hear then the parable of the sower. When any one hears the word of the kingdom and does not understand it, the evil one comes and snatches away what is sown in his heart; this is what was sown along the path. As for what was sown on rocky ground, this is he who hears the word and immediately receives it with joy; yet he has no root in himself, but endures for a while, and when tribulation or persecution arises on account of the word, immediately he falls away. As for what was sown among thorns, this is he who hears the word, but the cares of the world and the delight in riches choke the word, and it proves unfruitful. As for what was sown on good soil, this is he who hears the word and understands it; he indeed bears fruit, and yields, in one case a hundredfold, in another sixty, and in another thirty."

Mar 4:21-23 - And he said to them, "Is a lamp brought in to be put under a bushel, or under a bed, and not on a stand? For there is nothing hid, except to be made manifest; nor is anything secret, except to come to light. If any man has ears to hear, let him hear."

Mat 13:24-30 - Another parable he put before them, saying, "The kingdom of heaven may be compared to a man who sowed good seed in his field; but while men were sleeping, his enemy came and sowed weeds among the wheat, and went away. So when the plants came up and bore grain, then the weeds appeared also.

And the servants of the householder came and said to him, 'Sir, did you not sow good seed in your field? How then has it weeds?' He said to them, 'An enemy has done this.' The servants said to him, 'Then do you want us to go and gather them?' But he said, 'No; lest in gathering the weeds you root up the wheat along with them. Let both grow together until the harvest; and at harvest time I will tell the reapers, Gather the weeds first and bind them in bundles to be burned, but gather the wheat into my barn.'"

Mat 13:36-38 - Then he left the crowds and went into the house. And his disciples came to him, saying, "Explain to us the parable of the weeds of the field." He answered, "He who sows the good seed is the Son of man; the field is the world, and the good seed means the sons of the kingdom; the weeds are the sons of the evil one,

Mat 13:39-52 - and the enemy who sowed them is the devil; the harvest is the close of the age, and the reapers are angels. Just as the weeds are gathered and burned with fire, so will it be at the close of the age. The Son of man will send his angels, and they will gather out of his kingdom all causes of sin and all evildoers, and throw them into the furnace of fire; there men will weep and gnash their teeth. Then the righteous will shine like the sun in the kingdom of their Father. He who has ears, let him hear. "The kingdom of heaven is like treasure hidden in a field, which a man found and covered up; then in his joy he goes and sells all that he has and buys that field. "Again, the kingdom of heaven is like a merchant in search of fine pearls, who, on finding one pearl of great value, went and sold all that he had and bought it. "Again, the kingdom of heaven is like a net which was thrown into the sea and gathered fish of every kind; when it was full, men drew it ashore and sat down and sorted the good into vessels but threw away the bad. So it will be at the close of the age. The angels will come out and separate the evil from the righteous, and throw them into the furnace of fire; there men will weep and gnash their teeth. "Have you understood all this?" They said to him, "Yes." And he said to them, "Therefore every scribe who has been trained for the kingdom of heaven is like a householder who brings out of his treasure what is new and what is old."

Mar 4:26-34 - And he said, "The kingdom of God is as if a man should scatter seed upon the ground, and should sleep and rise night and day, and the seed should sprout and grow, he knows not how. The earth produces of itself, first the blade, then the ear, then the full grain in the ear. But when the grain is ripe, at once he puts in the sickle, because the harvest has come." And he said, "With what can we compare the kingdom of God, or what parable shall we use for it? It is like a grain of mustard seed, which, when sown upon the ground, is the smallest of all the seeds on earth; yet when it is sown it grows up and becomes the greatest of all shrubs, and puts forth large branches, so that the birds of the air can make nests in its shade." With many such parables he spoke the word to them, as they were able to hear it; he did not speak to them without a parable, but privately to his own disciples he explained everything.

Lu 9:57-62 - As they were going along the road, a man said to him, "I will follow you wherever you go." And Jesus said to him, "Foxes have holes, and birds of the air have nests; but the Son of man has nowhere to lay his head." To another he said, "Follow me." But he said, "Lord, let me first go and bury my father." But he said to him, "Leave the dead to bury their own dead; but as for you, go and proclaim the kingdom of God." Another said, "I will follow you, Lord; but let me first say farewell to those at my home." Jesus said to him, "No one who puts his hand to the plow and looks back is fit for the kingdom of God."

Lu 5:27-29 - After this he went out, and saw a tax collector, named Levi, sitting at the tax office; and he said to him, "Follow me." And he left everything, and rose and followed him. And Levi made him a great feast in his house; and there was a large company of tax collectors and others sitting at table with them.

Mar 2:15-17 - And as he sat at table in his house, many tax collectors and sinners were sitting with Jesus and his disciples; for there were many who followed him. And the scribes of the Pharisees, when they saw that he was eating with sinners and tax collectors, said to his disciples, "Why does he eat with tax collectors and sinners?" And when Jesus heard it, he said to them, "Those who are well have no need of a physician, but those who are sick; I came not to call the righteous, but sinners."

Lu 5:36-38 - He told them a parable also: "No one tears a piece from a new garment and puts it upon an old garment; if he does, he will tear the new, and the piece from the new will not match the old. And no one puts new wine into old wineskins; if he does, the new wine will burst the skins and it will be spilled, and the skins will be destroyed. But new wine must be put into fresh wineskins.

Mat 13:53-56 - And when Jesus had finished these parables, he went away from there, and coming to his own country he taught them in their synagogue, so that they were astonished, and said, "Where did this man get this wisdom and these mighty works? Is not this the carpenter's son? Is not his mother called Mary? And are not his brothers James and Joseph and Simon and Judas? And are not all his sisters with us? Where then did this man get all this?"

Mat 13:57 - And they took offense at him. But Jesus said to them, "A prophet is not without honor except in his own country and in his own house."

Mat 9:36 - When he saw the crowds, he had compassion for them, because they were harassed and helpless, like sheep without a shepherd.

Mar 6:7 - And he called to him the twelve, and began to send them out two by two, and gave them authority over the unclean spirits.

Mat 10:5-6 - These twelve Jesus sent out, charging them, "Go nowhere among the Gentiles, and enter no town of the Samaritans, but go rather to the lost sheep of the house of Israel.

Mat 10:9-17 - Take no gold, nor silver, nor copper in your belts, no bag for your journey, nor two tunics, nor sandals, nor a staff; for the laborer deserves his food. And whatever town or village you enter, find out who is worthy in it, and stay with him until you depart. As you enter the house, salute it. And if the house is worthy, let your peace come upon it; but if it is not worthy, let your peace return to you. And if anyone will not receive you or listen to your words, shake off the dust from your feet as you leave that house or town. Truly, I say to you, it shall be more tolerable on the day of judgment for the land of Sodom and Gomor'rah than for that town. "Behold, I send you out as sheep in the midst of wolves; so be wise as serpents and innocent as doves. Beware of men; for they will deliver you up to councils, and flog you in their synagogues,

Mat 10:18 - and you will be dragged before governors and kings for my sake, to bear testimony before them and the Gentiles.

Mat 10:23 - When they persecute you in one town, flee to the next; for truly, I say to you, you will not have gone through all the towns of Israel, before the Son of man comes.

Mat 10:26-31 - "So have no fear of them; for nothing is covered that will not be revealed, or hidden that will not be known. What I tell you in the dark, utter in the light; and what you hear whispered, proclaim upon the housetops. And do not fear those who kill the body but cannot kill the soul; rather fear him who can destroy both soul and body in hell. Are not two sparrows sold for a penny? And not one of them will fall to the ground without your Father's will. But even the hairs of your head are all numbered. Fear not, therefore; you are of more value than many sparrows.

Mar 6:12 - So they went out and preached that men should repent.

Mar 6:30 - The apostles returned to Jesus, and told him all that they had done and taught.

Mar 7:4-5 - and when they come from the market place, they do not eat unless they purify themselves; and there are many other traditions which they observe, the washing of cups and pots and vessels of bronze.) And the Pharisees and the scribes asked him, "Why do your disciples not live according to the tradition of the elders, but eat with hands defiled?"

Mar 7:14-24 - And he called the people to him again, and said to them, "Hear me, all of you, and understand: there is nothing outside a man which by going into him can defile him; but the things which come out of a man are what defile him." Other ancient authorities insert verse 16, ["If any man has ears to hear, let him hear."] And when he had entered the house, and left the people, his disciples asked him about the parable. And he said to them, "Then are you also without understanding? Do you not see that whatever goes into a man from outside cannot defile him, since it enters, not his heart but his stomach, and so passes on?" (Thus he declared all foods clean.) And he said, "What comes out of a man is what defiles a man. For from within, out of the heart of man, come evil thoughts, fornication, theft, murder, adultery, coveting, wickedness, deceit, licentiousness, envy, slander, pride, foolishness. All these evil things come from within, and they defile a man." And from there he arose and went away to the region of Tyre and Sidon. And he entered a house, and would not have any one know it; yet he could not be hid.

Mat 18:1-4 - At that time the disciples came to Jesus, saying, "Who is the greatest in the kingdom of heaven?" And calling to him a child, he put him in the midst of them, and said, "Truly, I say to you, unless you turn and become like children, you will never enter the kingdom of heaven. Whoever humbles himself like this child, he is the greatest in the kingdom of heaven.

Mat 18:7-9 - "Woe to the world for temptations to sin! For it is necessary that temptations come, but woe to the man by whom the temptation comes! And if your hand or your foot causes you to sin, cut it off and throw it away; it is better for you to enter life maimed or lame than with two hands or two feet to be thrown into the eternal fire. And if your eye causes you to sin, pluck it out and throw it away; it is better for you to enter life with one eye than with two eyes to be thrown into the hell of fire.

Mat 18:12-15 - What do you think? If a man has a hundred sheep, and one of them has gone astray, does he not leave the ninety-nine on the mountains and go in search of the one that went astray? And if he finds it, truly, I say to you, he rejoices over it more than over the ninety-nine that never went astray. So it is not the will of my Father who is in heaven that one of these little ones should perish. "If your brother sins against you, go and tell him his fault, between you and him alone. If he listens to you, you have gained your brother.

Mat 18:16-17 - But if he does not listen, take one or two others along with you, that every word may be confirmed by the evidence of two or three witnesses. If he refuses to listen to them, tell it to the church; and if he refuses to listen even to the church, let him be to you as a Gentile and a tax collector.

Mat 18:21-30 - Then Peter came up and said to him, "Lord, how often shall my brother sin against me, and I forgive him? As many as seven times?" Jesus said to him, "I do not say to you seven times, but seventy times seven. "Therefore, the kingdom of heaven may be compared to a king who wished to settle accounts with his servants. When he began the reckoning, one was brought to him who owed him ten thousand talents; and as he could not pay, his lord ordered him to be sold, with his wife and children and all that he had, and payment to be made. So the servant fell on his knees, imploring him, 'Lord, have patience with me, and I will pay you everything.' And out of pity for him the lord of that servant released him and forgave him the debt. But that same servant, as he went out, came upon one of his fellow servants who owed him a hundred denarii; and seizing him by the throat he said, 'Pay what you owe.' So, his fellow servant fell down and besought him, 'Have patience with me, and I will pay you.' He refused and went and put him in prison till he should pay the debt.

Mat 18:31-35 - When his fellow servants saw what had taken place, they were greatly distressed, and they went and reported to their lord all that had taken place. Then his lord summoned him and said to him, 'You wicked servant! I forgave you all that debt because you besought me; and should not you have had mercy on your fellow servant, as I had mercy on you?' And in anger his lord delivered him to the jailers, till he should pay all his debt. So also my heavenly Father will do to every one of you, if you do not forgive your brother from your heart."

Lu 10:1-8 - After this the Lord appointed seventy others, and sent them on ahead of him, two by two, into every town and place where he himself was about to come. And he said to them, "The harvest is plentiful, but the laborers are few; pray therefore the Lord of the harvest to send out laborers into his harvest. Go your way; behold, I send you out as lambs in the midst of wolves.

Carry no purse, no bag, no sandals; and salute no one on the road. Whatever house you enter, first say, 'Peace be to this house!' And if a son of peace is there, your peace shall rest upon him; but if not, it shall return to you. And remain in the same house, eating and drinking what they provide, for the laborer deserves his wages; do not go from house to house. Whenever you enter a town and they receive you, eat what is set before you;

Lu 10:10-12 - But whenever you enter a town and they do not receive you, go into its streets and say, 'Even the dust of your town that clings to our feet, we wipe off against you; nevertheless know this, that the kingdom of God has come near.' I tell you; it shall be more tolerable on that day for Sodom than for that town.

John 7:2-16 - Now the Jews' feast of Tabernacles was at hand. So, his brothers said to him, "Leave here and go to Judea, that your disciples may see the works you are doing. For no man works in secret if he seeks to be known openly. If you do these things, show yourself to the world." For even his brothers did not believe in him. Jesus said to them, "My time has not yet come, but your time is always here. The world cannot hate you, but it hates me because I testify of it that its works are evil. Go to the feast yourselves; I am not going up to this feast, for my time has not yet fully come." So saying, he remained in Galilee. But after his brothers had gone up to the feast, then he also went up, not publicly but in private. The Jews were looking for him at the feast, and saying, "Where is he?" And there was much muttering about him among the people. While some said, "He is a good man," others said, "No, he is leading the people astray." Yet for fear of the Jews no one spoke openly of him. About the middle of the feast Jesus went up into the temple and taught. The Jews marveled at it, saying, "How is it that this man has learning, when he has never studied?" So Jesus answered them, "My teaching is not mine, but his who sent me;

Jo 7:19-26 - Did not Moses give you the law? Yet none of you keeps the law. Why do you seek to kill me?" The people answered, "You have a demon! Who is seeking to kill you?" Jesus answered them, "I did one deed, and you all marvel at it. Moses gave you circumcision (not that it is from Moses, but from the fathers), and you circumcise a man upon the sabbath. If on the sabbath a man receives circumcision, so that the law of Moses may not be broken, are you angry with me because on the sabbath I made a man's whole body well? Do not judge by appearances, but judge with right judgment." Some of the people of Jerusalem therefore said, "Is not this the man whom they seek to kill? And here he is, speaking openly, and they say nothing to him! Can it be that the authorities really know that this is the Christ?

Jo 7:32 - The Pharisees heard the crowd thus muttering about him, and the chief priests and Pharisees sent officers to arrest him.

Jo 7:43-49 - So there was a division among the people over him. Some of them wanted to arrest him, but no one laid hands on him. The officers then went back to the chief priests and Pharisees, who said to them, "Why did you not bring him?" The officers answered, "No man ever spoke like this man!" The Pharisees answered them, "Are you led astray, you also? Have any of the authorities or of the Pharisees believed in him? But this crowd, who do not know the law, are accursed."

Jo 7:50-53 - Nicode'mus, who had gone to him before, and who was one of them, said to them, "Does our law judge a man without first giving him a hearing and learning what he does?" They replied, "Are you from Galilee too? Search and you will see that no prophet is to rise from Galilee." They went each to his own house,

Jo 8:1-11 - but Jesus went to the Mount of Olives. Early in the morning he came again to the temple; all the people came to him, and he sat down and taught them. The scribes and the Pharisees brought a woman who had been caught in adultery, and placing her in the midst they said to him, "Teacher, this woman has been caught in the act of adultery. Now in the law Moses commanded us to stone such. What do you say about her?" This they said to test him, that they might have some charge to bring against him. Jesus bent down and wrote with his finger on the ground. And as they continued to ask him, he stood up and said to them, "Let him who is without sin among you be the first to throw a stone at her." And once more he bent down and wrote with his finger on the ground. But when they heard it, they went away, one by one, beginning with the eldest, and Jesus was left alone with the woman standing before him. Jesus looked up and said to her, "Woman, where are they? Has no one condemned you?" She said, "No one, Lord." And Jesus said, "Neither do I condemn you; go, and do not sin again."

Jo 9:1-3 - As he passed by, he saw a man blind from his birth. And his disciples asked him, "Rabbi, who sinned, this man or his parents, that he was born blind?" Jesus answered, "It was not that this man sinned, or his parents, but that the works of God might be made manifest in him.

Jo 10:1-5 - "Truly, truly, I say to you, he who does not enter the sheepfold by the door but climbs in by another way, that man is a thief and a robber; but he who enters by the door is the shepherd of the sheep. To him the gatekeeper opens; the sheep hear his voice, and he calls his own sheep by name and leads them out. When he has brought out all his own, he goes before them, and the sheep follow him, for they know his voice. A stranger they will not follow, but they will flee from him, for they do not know the voice of strangers."

Jo 10:11-16 - I am the good shepherd. The good shepherd lays down his life for the sheep. He who is a hireling and not a shepherd, whose own the sheep are not, sees the wolf coming and leaves the sheep and flees; and the wolf snatches them and scatters them. He flees because he is a hireling and cares nothing for the sheep. I am the good shepherd; I know my own and my own know me, as the Father knows me and I know the Father; and I lay down my life for the sheep. And I have other sheep, that are not of this fold; I must bring them also, and they will heed my voice. So there shall be one flock, one shepherd.

Lu 10:25-37 - And behold, a lawyer stood up to put him to the test, saying, "Teacher, what shall I do to inherit eternal life?" He said to him, "What is written in the law? How do you read?" And he answered, "You shall love the Lord your God with all your heart, and with all your soul, and with all your strength, and with all your mind; and your neighbor as yourself." And he said to him, "You have answered right; do this, and you will live." But he, desiring to justify himself, said to Jesus, "And who is my neighbor?"

Jesus replied, "A man was going down from Jerusalem to Jericho, and he fell among robbers, who stripped him and beat him, and departed, leaving him half dead. Now by chance a priest was going down that road; and when he saw him, he passed by on the other side. So likewise, a Levite, when he came to the place and saw him, passed by on the other side. But a Samaritan, as he journeyed, came to where he was; and when he saw him, he had compassion, and went to him and bound up his wounds, pouring on oil and wine; then he set him on his own beast and brought him to an inn, and took care of him. And the next day he took out two denarii and gave them to the innkeeper, saying, 'Take care of him; and whatever more you spend, I will repay you when I come back.' Which of these three, do you think, proved neighbor to the man who fell among the robbers?" He said, "The one who showed mercy on him." And Jesus said to him, "Go and do likewise."

Lu 11:1-12 - He was praying in a certain place, and when he ceased, one of his disciples said to him, "Lord, teach us to pray, as John taught his disciples." And he said to them, "When you pray, say: "Father, hallowed be thy name. Thy kingdom come. Give us each day our daily bread; and forgive us our sins, for we ourselves forgive everyone who is indebted to us; and lead us not into temptation." And he said to them, "Which of you who has a friend will go to him at midnight and say to him, 'Friend, lend me three loaves; for a friend of mine has arrived on a journey, and I have nothing to set before him'; and he will answer from within, 'Do not bother me; the door is now shut, and my children are with me in bed; I cannot get up and give you anything'? I tell you, though he will not get up and give him anything because he is his friend, yet because of his importunity he will rise and give him whatever he needs. And I tell you, Ask, and it will be given you; seek, and you will find; knock, and it will be opened to you. For every one who asks receives, and he who seeks finds, and to him who knocks it will be opened. What father among you, if his son asks for a fish, will instead of a fish give him a serpent; or if he asks for an egg, will give him a scorpion?

Lu 11:13 - If you then, who are evil, know how to give good gifts to your children, how much more will the heavenly Father give the Holy Spirit to those who ask him!"

Lu 14:1-12 - One sabbath when he went to dine at the house of a ruler who belonged to the Pharisees, they were watching him. And behold, there was a man before him who had dropsy. And Jesus spoke to the lawyers and Pharisees, saying, "Is it lawful to heal on the sabbath, or not?" But they were silent. Then he took him and healed him, and let him go. And he said to them, "Which of you, having a son or an ox that has fallen into a well, will not immediately pull him out on a sabbath day?" And they could not reply to this. Now he told a parable to those who were invited, when he marked how they chose the places of honor, saying to them, "When you are invited by anyone to a marriage feast, do not sit down in a place of honor, lest a more eminent man than you be invited by him; and he who invited you both will come and say to you, 'Give place to this man,' and then you will begin with shame to take the lowest place. But when you are invited, go and sit in the lowest place, so that when your host comes, he may say to you, 'Friend, go up higher'; then you will be honored in the presence of all who sit at table with you. For every one who exalts himself will be humbled, and he who humbles himself will be exalted." He said also to the man who had invited him, "When you give a dinner or a banquet, do not invite your friends or your brothers or your kinsmen or rich neighbors, lest they also invite you in return, and you be repaid.

Lu 14:13-14 - But when you give a feast, invite the poor, the maimed, the lame, the blind, and you will be blessed, because they cannot repay you. You will be repaid at the resurrection of the just."

Lu 14:16-24 - But he said to him, "A man once gave a great banquet, and invited many; and at the time for the banquet he sent his servant to say to those who had been invited, 'Come; for all is now ready.' But they all alike began to make excuses. The first said to him, 'I have bought a field, and I must go out and see it; I pray you, have me excused.' And another said, 'I have bought five yoke of oxen, and I go to examine them; I pray you, have me excused.' And another said, 'I have married a wife, and therefore I cannot come.' So the servant came and reported this to his master. Then the householder in anger said to his servant, 'Go out quickly to the streets and lanes of the city, and bring in the poor and maimed and blind and lame.' And the servant said, 'Sir, what you commanded has been done, and still there is room.' And the master said to the servant, 'Go out to the highways and hedges, and compel people to come in, that my house may be filled. For I tell you, none of those men who were invited shall taste my banquet.'"

Lu 14:28-29 - For which of you, desiring to build a tower, does not first sit down and count the cost, whether he has enough to complete it? Otherwise, when he has laid a foundation, and is not able to finish, all who see it begin to mock him,

Lu 14:30-32 - saying, 'This man began to build, and was not able to finish.' Or what king, going to encounter another king in war, will not sit down first and take counsel whether he is able with ten thousand to meet him who comes against him with twenty thousand? And if not, while the other is yet a great way off, he sends an embassy and asks terms of peace.

Lu 15:1-10 - Now the tax collectors and sinners were all drawing near to hear him. And the Pharisees and the scribes murmured, saying, "This man receives sinners and eats with them." So, he told them this parable: "What man of you, having a hundred sheep, if he has lost one of them, does not leave the ninety-nine in the wilderness, and go after the one which is lost, until he finds it? And when he has found it, he lays it on his shoulders, rejoicing. And when he comes home, he calls together his friends and his neighbors, saying to them, 'Rejoice with me, for I have found my sheep which was lost.' Just so, I tell you, there will be more joy in heaven over one sinner who repents than over ninety-nine righteous persons who need no repentance. "Or what woman, having ten silver coins, if she loses one coin, does not light a lamp and sweep the house and seek diligently until she finds it? And when she has found it, she calls together her friends and neighbors, saying, 'Rejoice with me, for I have found the coin which I had lost.' Just so, I tell you, there is joy before the angels of God over one sinner who repents."

Lu 15:11-23 - And he said, "There was a man who had two sons; and the younger of them said to his father, 'Father, give me the

share of property that falls to me.' And he divided his living between them. Not many days later, the younger son gathered all he
had and took his journey into a far country, and there he squan-
dered his property in loose living. And when he had spent everything, a great famine arose in that country, and he began to be in
want. So he went and joined himself to one of the citizens of that
country, who sent him into his fields to feed swine. And he would
gladly have fed on the pods that the swine ate; and no one gave
him anything. But when he came to himself, he said, 'How many
of my father's hired servants have bread enough and to spare, but
I perish here with hunger! I will arise and go to my father, and I
will say to him, "Father, I have sinned against heaven and before
you; I am no longer worthy to be called your son; treat me as one
of your hired servants."' And he arose and came to his father. But
while he was yet at a distance, his father saw him and had compassion, and ran and embraced him and kissed him. And the son
said to him, 'Father, I have sinned against heaven and before you;
I am no longer worthy to be called your son.' But the father said
to his servants, 'Bring quickly the best robe, and put it on him; and
put a ring on his hand, and shoes on his feet; and bring the fatted
calf and kill it, and let us eat and make merry;

Lu 15:24-32 - for this my son was dead, and is alive again; he was
lost, and is found.' And they began to make merry. "Now his elder
son was in the field; and as he came and drew near to the house,
he heard music and dancing. And he called one of the servants
and asked what this meant. And he said to him, 'Your brother
has come, and your father has killed the fatted calf, because he
has received him safe and sound.' But he was angry and refused
to go in. His father came out and entreated him, but he answered
his father, 'Lo, these many years I have served you, and I never
disobeyed your command; yet you never gave me a kid, that I
might make merry with my friends. But when this son of yours
came, who has devoured your living with harlots, you killed for
him the fatted calf!' And he said to him, 'Son, you are always with
me, and all that is mine is yours. It was fitting to make merry and
be glad, for this your brother was dead, and is alive; he was lost,
and is found.'"

Lu 16:1-3 - He also said to the disciples, "There was a rich man who had a steward, and charges were brought to him that this man was wasting his goods. And he called him and said to him, 'What is this that I hear about you? Turn in the account of your stewardship, for you can no longer be steward.' And the steward said to himself, 'What shall I do, since my master is taking the stewardship away from me? I am not strong enough to dig, and I am ashamed to beg.

Lu 16:4-15 - I have decided what to do, so that people may receive me into their houses when I am put out of the stewardship.' So, summoning his master's debtors one by one, he said to the first, 'How much do you owe my master?' He said, 'A hundred measures of oil.' And he said to him, 'Take your bill, and sit down quickly and write fifty.' Then he said to another, 'And how much do you owe?' He said, 'A hundred measures of wheat.' He said to him, 'Take your bill, and write eighty.' The master commended the dishonest steward for his shrewdness; for the sons of this world are shrewder in dealing with their own generation than the sons of light. And I tell you, make friends for yourselves by means of unrighteous mammon, so that when it fails, they may receive you into the eternal habitations. "He who is faithful in a very little is faithful also in much; and he who is dishonest in a very little is dishonest also in much. If then you have not been faithful in the unrighteous mammon, who will entrust to you the true riches? And if you have not been faithful in that which is another's, who will give you that which is your own? No servant can serve two masters; for either he will hate the one and love the other, or he will be devoted to the one and despise the other. You cannot serve God and mammon." The Pharisees, who were lovers of money, heard all this, and they scoffed at him. But he said to them, "You are those who justify yourselves before men, but God knows your hearts; for what is exalted among men is an abomination in the sight of God.

Lu 16:18-29 - "Everyone who divorces his wife and marries another commits adultery, and he who marries a woman divorced from her husband commits adultery. "There was a rich man, who was clothed in purple and fine linen and who feasted sumptuously every day. And at his gate lay a poor man named Laz'arus, full of sores, who desired to be fed with what fell from the rich man's table; moreover, the dogs came and licked his sores. The poor man died and was carried by the angels to Abraham's bosom. The rich man also died and was buried; and in Hades, being in torment, he lifted up his eyes, and saw Abraham far off and Laz'arus in his bosom. And he called out, 'Father Abraham, have mercy upon me, and send Laz'arus to dip the end of his finger in water and cool my tongue; for I am in anguish in this flame.' But Abraham said, 'Son, remember that you in your lifetime received your good things, and Laz'arus in like manner evil things; but now he is comforted here, and you are in anguish. And besides all this, between us and you a great chasm has been fixed, in order that those who would pass from here to you may not be able, and none may cross from there to us.' And he said, 'Then I beg you, father, to send him to my father's house, for I have five brothers, so that he may warn them, lest they also come into this place of torment.' But Abraham said, 'They have Moses and the prophets; let them hear them.'

Lu 16:30-31 - And he said, 'No, father Abraham; but if someone goes to them from the dead, they will repent.' He said to him, 'If they do not hear Moses and the prophets, neither will they be convinced if someone should rise from the dead.'"

Lu 17:1-4 - And he said to his disciples, "Temptations to sin are sure to come; but woe to him by whom they come! It would be better for him if a millstone were hung round his neck and he were cast into the sea, than that he should cause one of these little ones to sin. Take heed to yourselves; if your brother sins, rebuke him, and if he repents, forgive him; and if he sins against you seven times in the day, and turns to you seven times, and says, 'I repent,' you must forgive him."

Lu 17:7-10 - "Will any one of you, who has a servant plowing or keeping sheep, say to him when he has come in from the field, 'Come at once and sit down at table'? Will he not rather say to him, 'Prepare supper for me, and gird yourself and serve me, till I eat and drink; and afterward you shall eat and drink'? Does he thank the servant because he did what was commanded? So, you also, when you have done all that is commanded you, say, 'We are unworthy servants; we have only done what was our duty.'"

Lu 17:20 - Being asked by the Pharisees when the kingdom of God was coming, he answered them, "The kingdom of God is not coming with signs to be observed;

Lu 17:26-36 - As it was in the days of Noah, so will it be in the days of the Son of man. They ate, they drank, they married, they were given in marriage, until the day when Noah entered the ark, and the flood came and destroyed them all. Likewise as it was in the days of Lot--they ate, they drank, they bought, they sold, they planted, they built, but on the day when Lot went out from Sodom fire and Sulphur rained from heaven and destroyed them all-- so will it be on the day when the Son of man is revealed. On that day, let him who is on the housetop, with his goods in the house, not come down to take them away; and likewise let him who is in the field not turn back. Remember Lot's wife. Whoever seeks to gain his life will lose it, but whoever loses his life will preserve it. I tell you, in that night there will be two in one bed; one will be taken and the other left. There will be two women grinding together; one will be taken and the other left." Other ancient authorities insert verse 36, ["Two men will be in the field; one will be taken and the other left."]

Lu 18:1-3 - And he told them a parable, to the effect that they ought always to pray and not lose heart. He said, "In a certain city there was a judge who neither feared God nor regarded man; and there was a widow in that city who kept coming to him and saying, 'Vindicate me against my adversary.'

Lu 18:4-14 - For a while he refused; but afterward he said to himself, 'Though I neither fear God nor regard man, yet because this widow bothers me, I will vindicate her, or she will wear me out by her continual coming.'" And the Lord said, "Hear what the unrighteous judge says. And will not God vindicate his elect, who cry to him day and night? Will he delay long over them? I tell you, he will vindicate them speedily. Nevertheless, when the Son of man comes, will he find faith on earth?" He also told this parable to some who trusted in themselves that they were righteous and despised others: "Two men went up into the temple to pray, one a Pharisee and the other a tax collector. The Pharisee stood and prayed thus with himself, 'God, I thank thee that I am not like other men, extortioners, unjust, adulterers, or even like this tax collector. I fast twice a week, I give tithes of all that I get.' But the tax collector, standing far off, would not even lift up his eyes to heaven, but beat his breast, saying, 'God, be merciful to me a sinner!' I tell you; this man went down to his house justified rather than the other; for everyone who exalts himself will be humbled, but he who humbles himself will be exalted."

Lu 10:38-40 - Now as they went on their way, he entered a village; and a woman named Martha received him into her house. And she had a sister called Mary, who sat at the Lord's feet and listened to his teaching. But Martha was distracted with much serving; and she went to him and said, "Lord, do you not care that my sister has left me to serve alone? Tell her then to help me."

Lu 10:41-42 - But the Lord answered her, "Martha, Martha, you are anxious and troubled about many things; one thing is needful. Mary has chosen the good portion, which shall not be taken away from her."

Mat 19:1-10 - Now when Jesus had finished these sayings, he went away from Galilee and entered the region of Judea beyond the Jordan; and large crowds followed him, and he healed them there. And Pharisees came up to him and tested him by asking, "Is it lawful to divorce one's wife for any cause?" He answered, "Have you not read that he who made them from the beginning made them male and female, and said, 'For this reason a man shall leave his father and mother and be joined to his wife, and the two shall become one flesh'? So they are no longer two but one flesh. What therefore God has joined together, let not man put asunder." They said to him, "Why then did Moses command one to give a certificate of divorce, and to put her away?" He said to them, "For your hardness of heart Moses allowed you to divorce your wives, but from the beginning it was not so. And I say to you: whoever divorces his wife, except for unchastity, and marries another, commits adultery." The disciples said to him, "If such is the case of a man with his wife, it is not expedient to marry."

Mat 19:11-25 - But he said to them, "Not all men can receive this saying, but only those to whom it is given. For there are eunuchs who have been so from birth, and there are eunuchs who have been made eunuchs by men, and there are eunuchs who have made themselves eunuchs for the sake of the kingdom of heaven. He who is able to receive this, let him receive it." Then children were brought to him that he might lay his hands on them and pray. The disciples rebuked the people; but Jesus said, "Let the children come to me, and do not hinder them; for to such belongs the kingdom of heaven." And he laid his hands on them and went away. And behold, one came up to him, saying, "Teacher, what good deed must I do, to have eternal life?" And he said to him, "Why do you ask me about what is good? One there is who is good. If you would enter life, keep the commandments." He said to him, "Which?" And Jesus said, "You shall not kill, You shall not commit adultery, You shall not steal, You shall not bear false witness, Honor your father and mother, and, You shall love your neighbor as yourself." The young man said to him, "All these I have observed; what do I still lack?" Jesus said to him, "If you would be perfect, go, sell what you possess and give to the poor, and you will have treasure in heaven; and come, follow me." When the young man heard this, he went away sorrowful; for he had great possessions. And Jesus said to his disciples, "Truly, I say to you, it will be hard for a rich man to enter the kingdom of heaven. Again, I tell you, it is easier for a camel to go through the eye of a needle than for a rich man to enter the kingdom of God." When the disciples heard this, they were greatly astonished, saying, "Who then can be saved?"

Mat 19:26 - But Jesus looked at them and said to them, "With men this is impossible, but with God all things are possible."

Mat 20:1-12 - "For the kingdom of heaven is like a householder who went out early in the morning to hire laborers for his vineyard. After agreeing with the laborers for a denarius a day, he sent them into his vineyard. And going out about the third hour he saw others standing idle in the market place; and to them he said, 'You go into the vineyard too, and whatever is right I will give you.' So, they went. Going out again about the sixth hour and the ninth hour, he did the same. And about the eleventh hour he went out and found others standing; and he said to them, 'Why do you stand here idle all day?' They said to him, 'Because no one has hired us.' He said to them, 'You go into the vineyard too.' And when evening came, the owner of the vineyard said to his steward, 'Call the laborers and pay them their wages, beginning with the last, up to the first.' And when those hired about the eleventh hour came, each of them received a denarius. Now when the first came, they thought they would receive more; but each of them also received a denarius. And on receiving it they grumbled at the householder, saying, 'These last worked only one hour, and you have made them equal to us who have borne the burden of the day and the scorching heat.'

Mat 20:13-16 - But he replied to one of them, 'Friend, I am doing you no wrong; did you not agree with me for a denarius? Take what belongs to you, and go; I choose to give to this last as I give to you. Am I not allowed to do what I choose with what belongs to me? Or do you begrudge my generosity?' So the last will be first, and the first last."

Lu 19:1-11 - He entered Jericho and was passing through. And there was a man named Zacchae'us; he was a chief tax collector, and rich. And he sought to see who Jesus was, but could not, on account of the crowd, because he was small of stature. So, he ran on ahead and climbed up into a sycamore tree to see him, for he was to pass that way. And when Jesus came to the place, he looked up and said to him, "Zacchae'us, make haste and come down; for I must stay at your house today." So, he made haste and came down, and received him joyfully. And when they saw it they all murmured, "He has gone in to be the guest of a man who is a sinner." And Zacchae'us stood and said to the Lord, "Behold, Lord, the half of my goods I give to the poor; and if I have defrauded any one of anything, I restore it fourfold." And Jesus said to him, "Today salvation has come to this house, since he also is a son of Abraham. For the Son of man came to seek and to save the lost." As they heard these things, he proceeded to tell a parable, because he was near to Jerusalem, and because they supposed that the kingdom of God was to appear immediately.

Lu 19:12-23 - He said therefore, "A nobleman went into a far country to receive a kingdom and then return. Calling ten of his servants, he gave them ten pounds, and said to them, 'Trade with these till I come.' But his citizens hated him and sent an embassy after him, saying, 'We do not want this man to reign over us.' When he returned, having received the kingdom, he commanded these servants, to whom he had given the money, to be called to him, that he might know what they had gained by trading. The first came before him, saying, 'Lord, your pound has made ten pounds more.' And he said to him, 'Well done, good servant! Because you have been faithful in a very little, you shall have authority over ten cities.' And the second came, saying, 'Lord, your pound has made five pounds.' And he said to him, 'And you are to be over five cities.' Then another came, saying, 'Lord, here is your pound, which I kept laid away in a napkin; for I was afraid of you, because you are a severe man; you take up what you did not lay down, and reap what you did not sow.' He said to him, 'I will condemn you out of your own mouth, you wicked servant! You knew that I was a severe man, taking up what I did not lay down and reaping what I did not sow? Why then did you not put my money into the bank, and at my coming I should have collected it with interest?'

Lu 19:24-28 - And he said to those who stood by, 'Take the pound from him, and give it to him who has the ten pounds.' (And they said to him, 'Lord, he has ten pounds!') 'I tell you, that to everyone who has will more be given; but from him who has not, even what he has will be taken away. But as for these enemies of mine, who did not want me to reign over them, bring them here and slay them before me.'" And when he had said this, he went on ahead, going up to Jerusalem.

Mat 21:1-3 - And when they drew near to Jerusalem and came to Beth'phage, to the Mount of Olives, then Jesus sent two disciples, saying to them, "Go into the village opposite you, and immediately you will find an ass tied, and a colt with her; untie them and bring them to me. If anyone says anything to you, you shall say, 'The Lord has need of them,' and he will send them immediately."

Mat 21:6-8 - The disciples went and did as Jesus had directed them; they brought the ass and the colt, and put their garments on them, and he sat thereon. Most of the crowd spread their garments on the road, and others cut branches from the trees and spread them on the road.

Mat 21:10 - And when he entered Jerusalem, all the city was stirred, saying, "Who is this?"

Jo 12:19-20 - The Pharisees then said to one another, "You see that you can do nothing; look, the world has gone after him." Now among those who went up to worship at the feast were some Greeks.

Jo 12:21-24 - So these came to Philip, who was from Beth-sa'ida in Galilee, and said to him, "Sir, we wish to see Jesus." Philip went and told Andrew; Andrew went with Philip and they told Jesus. And Jesus answered them, "The hour has come for the Son of man to be glorified. Truly, truly, I say to you, unless a grain of wheat falls into the earth and dies, it remains alone; but if it dies, it bears much fruit.

Mat 21:17 - And leaving them, he went out of the city to Bethany and lodged there.

Mar 11:12 - On the following day, when they came from Bethany, he was hungry.

Mar 11:15-19 - And they came to Jerusalem. And he entered the temple and began to drive out those who sold and those who bought in the temple, and he overturned the tables of the money-changers and the seats of those who sold pigeons; and he would not allow anyone to carry anything through the temple. And he taught, and said to them, "Is it not written, 'My house shall be called a house of prayer for all the nations'? But you have made it a den of robbers." And the chief priests and the scribes heard it and sought a way to destroy him; for they feared him, because all the multitude was astonished at his teaching. And when evening came, they went out of the city.

Mar 11:27 - And they came again to Jerusalem. And as he was walking in the temple, the chief priests and the scribes and the elders came to him,

Mat 21:28-31 - "What do you think? A man had two sons; and he went to the first and said, 'Son, go and work in the vineyard today.' And he answered, 'I will not'; but afterward he repented and went. And he went to the second and said the same; and he answered, 'I go, sir,' but did not go. Which of the two did the will of his father?" They said, "The first." Jesus said to them, "Truly, I say to you, the tax collectors and the harlots go into the kingdom of God before you.

Mat 21:33 - "Hear another parable. There was a householder who planted a vineyard, and set a hedge around it, and dug a wine press in it, and built a tower, and let it out to tenants, and went into another country.

Mar 12:1-9 - And he began to speak to them in parables. "A man planted a vineyard, and set a hedge around it, and dug a pit for the wine press, and built a tower, and let it out to tenants, and went into another country. When the time came, he sent a servant to the tenants, to get from them some of the fruit of the vineyard. And they took him and beat him, and sent him away empty-handed. Again he sent to them another servant, and they wounded him in the head, and treated him shamefully. And he sent another, and him they killed; and so with many others, some they beat and some they killed. He had still one other, a beloved son; finally, he sent him to them, saying, 'They will respect my son.' But those tenants said to one another, 'This is the heir; come, let us kill him, and the inheritance will be ours.' And they took him and killed him, and cast him out of the vineyard. What will the owner of the vineyard do? He will come and destroy the tenants, and give the vineyard to others.

Mat 21:45-46 - When the chief priests and the Pharisees heard his parables, they perceived that he was speaking about them. But when they tried to arrest him, they feared the multitudes, because they held him to be a prophet.

at 22:1-3 - And again Jesus spoke to them in parables, saying, "The kingdom of heaven may be compared to a king who gave a marriage feast for his son, and sent his servants to call those who were invited to the marriage feast; but they would not come.

Mat 22:4-18 - Again he sent other servants, saying, 'Tell those who are invited, Behold, I have made ready my dinner, my oxen and my fat calves are killed, and everything is ready; come to the marriage feast.' But they made light of it and went off, one to his farm, another to his business, while the rest seized his servants, treated them shamefully, and killed them. The king was angry, and he sent his troops and destroyed those murderers and burned their city. Then he said to his servants, 'The wedding is ready, but those invited were not worthy. Go therefore to the thoroughfares, and invite to the marriage feast as many as you find.' And those servants went out into the streets and gathered all whom they found, both bad and good; so the wedding hall was filled with guests. "But when the king came in to look at the guests, he saw there a man who had no wedding garment; and he said to him, 'Friend, how did you get in here without a wedding garment?' And he was speechless. Then the king said to the attendants, 'Bind him hand and foot, and cast him into the outer darkness; there men will weep and gnash their teeth.' For many are called, but few are chosen." Then the Pharisees went and took counsel how to entangle him in his talk. And they sent their disciples to him, along with the Hero'di-ans, saying, "Teacher, we know that you are true, and teach the way of God truthfully, and care for no man; for you do not regard the position of men. Tell us, then, what you think. Is it lawful to pay taxes to Caesar, or not?" But Jesus, aware of their malice, said, "Why put me to the test, you hypocrites?

Mat 22:19-33 - Show me the money for the tax." And they brought him a coin. And Jesus said to them, "Whose likeness and inscription is this?" They said, "Caesar's." Then he said to them, "Render therefore to Caesar the things that are Caesar's, and to God the things that are God's." When they heard it, they marveled; and they left him and went away. The same day Sad'ducees came to him, who say that there is no resurrection; and they asked him a question, saying, "Teacher, Moses said, 'If a man dies, having no children, his brother must marry the widow, and raise up children for his brother.' Now there were seven brothers among us; the first married, and died, and having no children left his wife to his brother. So too the second and third, down to the seventh. After them all, the woman died. In the resurrection, therefore, to which of the seven will she be wife? For they all had her." But Jesus answered them, "You are wrong, because you know neither the scriptures nor the power of God. For in the resurrection they neither marry nor are given in marriage, but are like angels in heaven. And as for the resurrection of the dead, have you not read what was said to you by God, 'I am the God of Abraham, and the God of Isaac, and the God of Jacob'? He is not God of the dead, but of the living." And when the crowd heard it, they were astonished at his teaching.

Mar 12:28-31 - And one of the scribes came up and heard them disputing with one another, and seeing that he answered them well, asked him, "Which commandment is the first of all?" Jesus answered, "The first is, 'Hear, O Israel: The Lord our God, the Lord is one; and you shall love the Lord your God with all your heart, and with all your soul, and with all your mind, and with all your strength.' The second is this, 'You shall love your neighbor as yourself.' There is no other commandment greater than these."

Mat 22:40 - On these two commandments depend all the law and the prophets."

Mar 12:32-33 - And the scribe said to him, "You are right, Teacher; you have truly said that he is one, and there is no other but he; and to love him with all the heart, and with all the understanding, and with all the strength, and to love one's neighbor as oneself, is much more than all whole burnt offerings and sacrifices."

Mat 23:1-6 - Then said Jesus to the crowds and to his disciples, "The scribes and the Pharisees sit on Moses' seat; so practice and observe whatever they tell you, but not what they do; for they preach, but do not practice. They bind heavy burdens, hard to bear, and lay them on men's shoulders; but they themselves will not move them with their finger. They do all their deeds to be seen by men; for they make their phylacteries broad and their fringes long, and they love the place of honor at feasts and the best seats in the synagogues,

Mat 23:7-19 - and salutations in the market places, and being called rabbi by men. But you are not to be called rabbi, for you have one teacher, and you are all brethren. And call no man your father on earth, for you have one Father, who is in heaven. Neither be called masters, for you have one master, the Christ. He who is greatest among you shall be your servant; whoever exalts himself will be humbled, and whoever humbles himself will be exalted. "But woe to you, scribes and Pharisees, hypocrites! because you shut the kingdom of heaven against men; for you neither enter yourselves, nor allow those who would enter to go in. Other ancient authorities here (or after verse 12) verse 14, [Woe to you, scribes and Pharisees, hypocrites! for you devour widows' houses and for a pretense you make long prayers; therefore, you will receive the greater condemnation.] Woe to you, scribes and Pharisees, hypocrites! for you traverse sea and land to make a single proselyte, and when he becomes a proselyte, you make him twice as much a child of hell as yourselves. "Woe to you, blind guides, who say, 'If any one swears by the temple, it is nothing; but if any one swears by the gold of the temple, he is bound by his oath.' You blind fools! For which is greater, the gold or the temple that has made the gold sacred? And you say, 'If any one swears by the altar, it is nothing; but if any one swears by the gift that is on the altar, he is bound by his oath.' You blind men! For which is greater, the gift or the altar that makes the gift sacred?

Mat 23:20-33 - So he who swears by the altar, swears by it and by everything on it; and he who swears by the temple, swears by it and by him who dwells in it; and he who swears by heaven, swears by the throne of God and by him who sits upon it. "Woe to you, scribes and Pharisees, hypocrites! for you tithe mint and dill and cummin, and have neglected the weightier matters of the law, justice and mercy and faith; these you ought to have done, without neglecting the others. You blind guides, straining out a gnat and swallowing a camel! "Woe to you, scribes and Pharisees, hypocrites! for you cleanse the outside of the cup and of the plate, but inside they are full of extortion and rapacity. You blind Pharisee! first cleanse the inside of the cup and of the plate, that the outside also may be clean. "Woe to you, scribes and Pharisees, hypocrites! for you are like whitewashed tombs, which outwardly appear beautiful, but within they are full of dead men's bones and all uncleanness. So you also outwardly appear righteous to men, but within you are full of hypocrisy and iniquity. "Woe to you, scribes and Pharisees, hypocrites! for you build the tombs of the prophets and adorn the monuments of the righteous, saying, 'If we had lived in the days of our fathers, we would not have taken part with them in shedding the blood of the prophets.' Thus you witness against yourselves, that you are sons of those who murdered the prophets. Fill up, then, the measure of your fathers. You serpents, you brood of vipers, how are you to escape being sentenced to hell?

Mar 12:41-44 - And he sat down opposite the treasury, and watched the multitude putting money into the treasury. Many rich people put in large sums. And a poor widow came, and put in two copper coins, which make a penny. And he called his disciples to him, and said to them, "Truly, I say to you, this poor widow has put in more than all those who are contributing to the treasury. For they all contributed out of their abundance; but she out of her poverty has put in everything she had, her whole living."

Mat 24:1-2 - Jesus left the temple and was going away, when his disciples came to point out to him the buildings of the temple. But he answered them, "You see all these, do you not? Truly, I say to you, there will not be left here one stone upon another, that will not be thrown down."

Mat 24:16-21 - then let those who are in Judea flee to the mountains; let him who is on the housetop not go down to take what is in his house; and let him who is in the field not turn back to take his mantle. And alas for those who are with child and for those who give suck in those days! Pray that your flight may not be in winter or on a sabbath. For then there will be great tribulation, such as has not been from the beginning of the world until now, no, and never will be.

Mat 24:29 - "Immediately after the tribulation of those days the sun will be darkened, and the moon will not give its light, and the stars will fall from heaven, and the powers of the heavens will be shaken;

Mat 24:32-33 - "From the fig tree learn its lesson: as soon as its branch becomes tender and puts forth its leaves, you know that summer is near. So also, when you see all these things, you know that he is near, at the very gates.

Mat 24:36-49 - "But of that day and hour no one knows, not even the angels of heaven, nor the Son, but the Father only. As were the days of Noah, so will be the coming of the Son of man. For as in those days before the flood they were eating and drinking, marrying and giving in marriage, until the day when Noah entered the ark, and they did not know until the flood came and swept them all away, so will be the coming of the Son of man. Then two men will be in the field; one is taken and one is left. Two women will be grinding at the mill; one is taken and one is left. Watch therefore, for you do not know on what day your Lord is coming. But know this, that if the householder had known in what part of the night the thief was coming, he would have watched and would not have let his house be broken into. Therefore, you also must be ready; for the Son of man is coming at an hour you do not expect. "Who then is the faithful and wise servant, whom his master has set over his household, to give them their food at the proper time? Blessed is that servant whom his master when he comes will find so doing. Truly, I say to you, he will set him over all his possessions. But if that wicked servant says to himself, 'My master is delayed,' and begins to beat his fellow servants, and eats and drinks with the drunken,

Mat 24:50-51 - the master of that servant will come on a day when he does not expect him and at an hour he does not know, and will punish him, and put him with the hypocrites; there men will weep and gnash their teeth.

Mat 25:1-15 - "Then the kingdom of heaven shall be compared to ten maidens who took their lamps and went to meet the bridegroom. Five of them were foolish, and five were wise. For when the foolish took their lamps, they took no oil with them; but the wise took flasks of oil with their lamps. As the bridegroom was delayed, they all slumbered and slept. But at midnight there was a cry, 'Behold, the bridegroom! Come out to meet him.' Then all those maidens rose and trimmed their lamps. And the foolish said to the wise, 'Give us some of your oil, for our lamps are going out.' But the wise replied, 'Perhaps there will not be enough for us and for you; go rather to the dealers and buy for yourselves.' And while they went to buy, the bridegroom came, and those who were ready went in with him to the marriage feast; and the door was shut. Afterward the other maidens came also, saying, 'Lord, lord, open to us.' But he replied, 'Truly, I say to you, I do not know you.' Watch therefore, for you know neither the day nor the hour. "For it will be as when a man going on a journey called his servants and entrusted to them his property; to one he gave five talents, to another two, to another one, to each according to his ability. Then he went away.

Mat 25:16-26 - He who had received the five talents went at once and traded with them; and he made five talents more. So also, he who had the two talents made two talents more. But he who had received the one talent went and dug in the ground and hid his master's money. Now after a long time the master of those servants came and settled accounts with them. And he who had received the five talents came forward, bringing five talents more, saying, 'Master, you delivered to me five talents; here I have made five talents more.' His master said to him, 'Well done, good and faithful servant; you have been faithful over a little, I will set you over much; enter into the joy of your master.' And he also who had the two talents came forward, saying, 'Master, you delivered to me two talents; here I have made two talents more.' His master said to him, 'Well done, good and faithful servant; you have been faithful over a little, I will set you over much; enter into the joy of your master.' He also who had received the one talent came forward, saying, 'Master, I knew you to be a hard man, reaping where you did not sow, and gathering where you did not winnow; so I was afraid, and I went and hid your talent in the ground. Here you have what is yours.' But his master answered him, 'You wicked and slothful servant! You knew that I reap where I have not sowed, and gather where I have not winnowed?

Mat 25:27-30 - Then you ought to have invested my money with the bankers, and at my coming I should have received what was my own with interest. So, take the talent from him, and give it to him who has the ten talents. For to everyone who has will more be given, and he will have abundance; but from him who has not, even what he has will be taken away. And cast the worthless servant into the outer darkness; there men will weep and gnash their teeth.'

Lu 21:34-36 - "But take heed to yourselves lest your hearts be weighed down with dissipation and drunkenness and cares of this life, and that day come upon you suddenly like a snare; for it will come upon all who dwell upon the face of the whole earth. But watch at all times, praying that you may have strength to escape all these things that will take place, and to stand before the Son of man."

Mat 25:31-36 - "When the Son of man comes in his glory, and all the angels with him, then he will sit on his glorious throne. Before him will be gathered all the nations, and he will separate them one from another as a shepherd separates the sheep from the goats, and he will place the sheep at his right hand, but the goats at the left. Then the King will say to those at his right hand, 'Come, O blessed of my Father, inherit the kingdom prepared for you from the foundation of the world; for I was hungry and you gave me food, I was thirsty and you gave me drink, I was a stranger and you welcomed me, I was naked and you clothed me, I was sick and you visited me, I was in prison and you came to me.'

Mat 25:37-46 - Then the righteous will answer him, 'Lord, when did we see thee hungry and feed thee, or thirsty and give thee drink? And when did we see thee a stranger and welcome thee, or naked and clothe thee? And when did we see thee sick or in prison and visit thee?' And the King will answer them, 'Truly, I say to you, as you did it to one of the least of these my brethren, you did it to me.' Then he will say to those at his left hand, 'Depart from me, you cursed, into the eternal fire prepared for the devil and his angels; for I was hungry and you gave me no food, I was thirsty and you gave me no drink, I was a stranger and you did not welcome me, naked and you did not clothe me, sick and in prison and you did not visit me.' Then they also will answer, 'Lord, when did we see thee hungry or thirsty or a stranger or naked or sick or in prison, and did not minister to thee?' Then he will answer them, 'Truly, I say to you, as you did it not to one of the least of these, you did it not to me.' And they will go away into eternal punishment, but the righteous into eternal life."

Mar 14:1-3 - It was now two days before the Passover and the feast of Unleavened Bread. And the chief priests and the scribes were seeking how to arrest him by stealth, and kill him; for they said, "Not during the feast, lest there be a tumult of the people." And while he was at Bethany in the house of Simon the leper, as he sat at table, a woman came with an alabaster flask of ointment of pure nard, very costly, and she broke the flask and poured it over his head.

Mar 14:4-8 - But there were some who said to themselves indignantly, "Why was the ointment thus wasted? For this ointment might have been sold for more than three hundred denarii, and given to the poor." And they reproached her. But Jesus said, "Let her alone; why do you trouble her? She has done a beautiful thing to me. For you always have the poor with you, and whenever you will, you can do good to them; but you will not always have me. She has done what she could; she has anointed my body beforehand for burying.

Mat 26:14-20 - Then one of the twelve, who was called Judas Iscariot, went to the chief priests and said, "What will you give me if I deliver him to you?" And they paid him thirty pieces of silver. And from that moment he sought an opportunity to betray him. Now on the first day of Unleavened Bread the disciples came to Jesus, saying, "Where will you have us prepare for you to eat the Passover?" He said, "Go into the city to a certain one, and say to him, 'The Teacher says, My time is at hand; I will keep the Passover at your house with my disciples.'" And the disciples did as Jesus had directed them, and they prepared the Passover. When it was evening, he sat at table with the twelve disciples;

Lu 22:24-25 - A dispute also arose among them, which of them was to be regarded as the greatest. And he said to them, "The kings of the Gentiles exercise lordship over them; and those in authority over them are called benefactors.

Lu 22:26-27 - But not so with you; rather let the greatest among you become as the youngest, and the leader as one who serves. For which is the greater, one who sits at table, or one who serves? Is it not the one who sits at table? But I am among you as one who serves.

Jo 13:2 - And during supper, when the devil had already put it into the heart of Judas Iscariot, Simon's son, to betray him,

Jo 13:4-17 - rose from supper, laid aside his garments, and girded himself with a towel. Then he poured water into a basin, and began to wash the disciples' feet, and to wipe them with the towel with which he was girded. He came to Simon Peter; and Peter said to him, "Lord, do you wash my feet?" Jesus answered him, "What I am doing you do not know now, but afterward you will understand." Peter said to him, "You shall never wash my feet." Jesus answered him, "If I do not wash you, you have no part in me." Simon Peter said to him, "Lord, not my feet only but also my hands and my head!" Jesus said to him, "He who has bathed does not need to wash, except for his feet, but he is clean all over; and you are clean, but not every one of you." For he knew who was to betray him; that was why he said, "You are not all clean." When he had washed their feet, and taken his garments, and resumed his place, he said to them, "Do you know what I have done to you? You call me Teacher and Lord; and you are right, for so I am. If I then, your Lord and Teacher, have washed your feet, you also ought to wash one another's feet. For I have given you an example, that you also should do as I have done to you. Truly, truly, I say to you, a servant is not greater than his master; nor is he who is sent greater than he who sent him. If you know these things, blessed are you if you do them.

Jo 13:21-26 - When Jesus had thus spoken, he was troubled in spirit, and testified, "Truly, truly, I say to you, one of you will betray me." The disciples looked at one another, uncertain of whom he spoke. One of his disciples, whom Jesus loved, was lying close to the breast of Jesus; so, Simon Peter beckoned to him and said, "Tell us who it is of whom he speaks." So lying thus, close to the breast of Jesus, he said to him, "Lord, who is it?" Jesus answered, "It is he to whom I shall give this morsel when I have dipped it." So, when he had dipped the morsel, he gave it to Judas, the son of Simon Iscariot.

Jo 13:31 - When he had gone out, Jesus said, "Now is the Son of man glorified, and in him God is glorified;

Jo 13:34-35 - A new commandment I give to you, that you love one another; even as I have loved you, that you also love one another. By this all men will know that you are my disciples, if you have love for one another."

Mat 26:31 - Then Jesus said to them, "You will all fall away because of me this night; for it is written, 'I will strike the shepherd, and the sheep of the flock will be scattered.'

Mat 26:33 - Peter declared to him, "Though they all fall away because of you, I will never fall away."

Lu 22:33-34 - And he said to him, "Lord, I am ready to go with you to prison and to death." He said, "I tell you, Peter, the cock will not crow this day, until you three times deny that you know me."

Mat 26:35-36 - Peter said to him, "Even if I must die with you, I will not deny you." And so said all the disciples. Then Jesus went with them to a place called Gethsem'ane, and he said to his disciples, "Sit here, while I go yonder and pray."

Mat 26:37-45 - And taking with him Peter and the two sons of Zeb'edee, he began to be sorrowful and troubled. Then he said to them, "My soul is very sorrowful, even to death; remain here, and watch with me." And going a little farther he fell on his face and prayed, "My Father, if it be possible, let this cup pass from me; nevertheless, not as I will, but as thou wilt." And he came to the disciples and found them sleeping; and he said to Peter, "So, could you not watch with me one hour? Watch and pray that you may not enter into temptation; the spirit indeed is willing, but the flesh is weak." Again, for the second time, he went away and prayed, "My Father, if this cannot pass unless I drink it, thy will be done." And again, he came and found them sleeping, for their eyes were heavy. So, leaving them again, he went away and prayed for the third time, saying the same words. Then he came to the disciples and said to them, "Are you still sleeping and taking your rest? Behold, the hour is at hand, and the Son of man is betrayed into the hands of sinners.

Jo 18:1-3 - When Jesus had spoken these words, he went forth with his disciples across the Kidron valley, where there was a garden, which he and his disciples entered. Now Judas, who betrayed him, also knew the place; for Jesus often met there with his disciples. So, Judas, procuring a band of soldiers and some officers from the chief priests and the Pharisees, went there with lanterns and torches and weapons.

Mat 26:48-50 - Now the betrayer had given them a sign, saying, "The one I shall kiss is the man; seize him." And he came up to Jesus at once and said, "Hail, Master!" And he kissed him. Jesus said to him, "Friend, why are you here?" Then they came up and laid hands on Jesus and seized him.

Jo 18:4-8 - Then Jesus, knowing all that was to befall him, came forward and said to them, "Whom do you seek?" They answered him, "Jesus of Nazareth." Jesus said to them, "I am he." Judas, who betrayed him, was standing with them. When he said to them, "I am he," they drew back and fell to the ground. Again he asked them, "Whom do you seek?" And they said, "Jesus of Nazareth." Jesus answered, "I told you that I am he; so, if you seek me, let these men go."

Mat 26:50-52 - Jesus said to him, "Friend, why are you here?" Then they came up and laid hands on Jesus and seized him. And behold, one of those who were with Jesus stretched out his hand and drew his sword, and struck the slave of the high priest, and cut off his ear. Then Jesus said to him, "Put your sword back into its place; for all who take the sword will perish by the sword.

Mat 26:55-56 - At that hour Jesus said to the crowds, "Have you come out as against a robber, with swords and clubs to capture me? Day after day I sat in the temple teaching, and you did not seize me. But all this has taken place, that the scriptures of the prophets might be fulfilled." Then all the disciples forsook him and fled.

Mar 14:51-52 - And a young man followed him, with nothing but a linen cloth about his body; and they seized him, but he left the linen cloth and ran away naked.

Mat 26:57 - Then those who had seized Jesus led him to Ca'iaphas the high priest, where the scribes and the elders had gathered.

Jo 18:15-16 - Simon Peter followed Jesus, and so did another disciple. As this disciple was known to the high priest, he entered the court of the high priest along with Jesus, while Peter stood outside at the door. So the other disciple, who was known to the high priest, went out and spoke to the maid who kept the door, and brought Peter in.

Jo 18:18 - Now the servants and officers had made a charcoal fire, because it was cold, and they were standing and warming themselves; Peter also was with them, standing and warming himself.

Jo 18:17 - The maid who kept the door said to Peter, "Are not you also one of this man's disciples?" He said, "I am not."

Jo 18:25-27 - Now Simon Peter was standing and warming himself. They said to him, "Are not you also one of his disciples?" He denied it and said, "I am not." One of the servants of the high priest, a kinsman of the man whose ear Peter had cut off, asked, "Did I not see you in the garden with him?" Peter again denied it; and at once the cock crowed.

Mat 26:75 - And Peter remembered the saying of Jesus, "Before the cock crows, you will deny me three times." And he went out and wept bitterly.

Jo 18:19-20 - The high priest then questioned Jesus about his disciples and his teaching. Jesus answered him, "I have spoken openly to the world; I have always taught in synagogues and in the temple, where all Jews come together; I have said nothing secretly.

Jo 18:21-23 - Why do you ask me? Ask those who have heard me, what I said to them; they know what I said." When he had said this, one of the officers standing by struck Jesus with his hand, saying, "Is that how you answer the high priest?" Jesus answered him, "If I have spoken wrongly, bear witness to the wrong; but if I have spoken rightly, why do you strike me?"

Mar 14:53 - And they led Jesus to the high priest; and all the chief priests and the elders and the scribes were assembled.

Mar 14:55-61 - Now the chief priests and the whole council sought testimony against Jesus to put him to death; but they found none.

For many bore false witness against him, and their witness did not agree. And some stood up and bore false witness against him, saying, "We heard him say, 'I will destroy this temple that is made with hands, and in three days I will build another, not made with hands.'" Yet not even so did their testimony agree. And the high priest stood up in the midst, and asked Jesus, "Have you no answer to make? What is it that these men testify against you?" But he was silent and made no answer. Again, the high priest asked him, "Are you the Christ, the Son of the Blessed?"

Lu 22:67-68 - "If you are the Christ, tell us." But he said to them, "If I tell you, you will not believe; and if I ask you, you will not answer.

Lu 22:70 - And they all said, "Are you the Son of God, then?" And he said to them, "You say that I am."

Mar 14:63-64 - And the high priest tore his garments, and said, "Why do we still need witnesses? You have heard his blasphemy. What is your decision?" And they all condemned him as deserving death.

Mar 14:65 - And some began to spit on him, and to cover his face, and to strike him, saying to him, "Prophesy!" And the guards received him with blows.

Jo 18:28-31 - Then they led Jesus from the house of Ca'iaphas to the praetorium. It was early. They themselves did not enter the praetorium, so that they might not be defiled, but might eat the Passover. So, Pilate went out to them and said, "What accusation do you bring against this man?" They answered him, "If this man were not an evildoer, we would not have handed him over." Pilate said to them, "Take him yourselves and judge him by your own law." The Jews said to him, "It is not lawful for us to put any man to death."

Jo 18:33-38 - Pilate entered the praetorium again and called Jesus, and said to him, "Are you the King of the Jews?" Jesus answered, "Do you say this of your own accord, or did others say it to you about me?" Pilate answered, "Am I a Jew? Your own nation and the chief priests have handed you over to me; what have you done?" Jesus answered, "My kingship is not of this world; if my kingship were of this world, my servants would fight, that I might not be handed over to the Jews; but my kingship is not from the world." Pilate said to him, "So you are a king?" Jesus answered, "You say that I am a king. For this I was born, and for this I have come into the world, to bear witness to the truth. Every one who is of the truth hears my voice." Pilate said to him, "What is truth?" After he had said this, he went out to the Jews again, and told them, "I find no crime in him.

Lu 23:5 - But they were urgent, saying, "He stirs up the people, teaching throughout all Judea, from Galilee even to this place."

Mat 27:13 - Then Pilate said to him, "Do you not hear how many things they testify against you?"

Lu 23:6-16 - When Pilate heard this, he asked whether the man was a Galilean. And when he learned that he belonged to Herod's jurisdiction, he sent him over to Herod, who was himself in Jerusalem at that time. When Herod saw Jesus, he was very glad, for he had long desired to see him, because he had heard about him, and he was hoping to see some sign done by him. So he questioned him at some length; but he made no answer. The chief priests and the scribes stood by, vehemently accusing him. And Herod with his soldiers treated him with contempt and mocked him; then, arraying him in gorgeous apparel, he sent him back to Pilate. And Herod and Pilate became friends with each other that very day, for before this they had been at enmity with each other. Pilate then called together the chief priests and the rulers and the people, and said to them, "You brought me this man as one who was perverting the people; and after examining him before you, behold, I did not find this man guilty of any of your charges against him; neither did Herod, for he sent him back to us. Behold, nothing deserving death has been done by him; I will therefore chastise him and release him."

Mat 27:15-23 - Now at the feast the governor was accustomed to release for the crowd any one prisoner whom they wanted. And they had then a notorious prisoner, called Barab'bas. So when they had gathered, Pilate said to them, "Whom do you want me to release for you, Barab'bas or Jesus who is called Christ?" For he knew that it was out of envy that they had delivered him up. Besides, while he was sitting on the judgment seat, his wife sent word to him, "Have nothing to do with that righteous man, for I have suffered much over him today in a dream." Now the chief priests and the elders persuaded the people to ask for Barab'bas and destroy Jesus. The governor again said to them, "Which of the two do you want me to release for you?" And they said, "Barab'bas." Pilate said to them, "Then what shall I do with Jesus who is called Christ?" They all said, "Let him be crucified." And he said, "Why, what evil has he done?" But they shouted all the more, "Let him be crucified."

Mat 27:26-27 - Then he released for them Barab'bas, and having scourged Jesus, delivered him to be crucified. Then the soldiers of the governor took Jesus into the praetorium, and they gathered the whole battalion before him.

Mat 27:29-31 - and plaiting a crown of thorns they put it on his head, and put a reed in his right hand. And kneeling before him they mocked him, saying, "Hail, King of the Jews!" And they spat upon him, and took the reed and struck him on the head. And when they had mocked him, they stripped him of the robe, and put his own clothes on him, and led him away to crucify him.

Mat 27:3-8 - When Judas, his betrayer, saw that he was condemned, he repented and brought back the thirty pieces of silver to the chief priests and the elders, saying, "I have sinned in betraying innocent blood." They said, "What is that to us? See to it yourself." And throwing down the pieces of silver in the temple, he departed; and he went and hanged himself. But the chief priests, taking the pieces of silver, said, "It is not lawful to put them into the treasury, since they are blood money." So, they took counsel, and bought with them the potter's field, to bury strangers in. Therefore that field has been called the Field of Blood to this day.

Lu 23:26-32 - And as they led him away, they seized one Simon of Cyre'ne, who was coming in from the country, and laid on him the cross, to carry it behind Jesus. And there followed him a great multitude of the people, and of women who bewailed and lamented him. But Jesus turning to them said, "Daughters of Jerusalem, do not weep for me, but weep for yourselves and for your children. For behold, the days are coming when they will say, 'Blessed are the barren, and the wombs that never bore, and the breasts that never gave suck!' Then they will begin to say to the mountains, 'Fall on us'; and to the hills, 'Cover us.' For if they do this when the wood is green, what will happen when it is dry?" Two others also, who were criminals, were led away to be put to death with him.

Jo 19:17-24 - So they took Jesus, and he went out, bearing his own cross, to the place called the place of a skull, which is called in Hebrew Gol'gotha. There they crucified him, and with him two others, one on either side, and Jesus between them. Pilate also wrote a title and put it on the cross; it read, "Jesus of Nazareth, the King of the Jews." Many of the Jews read this title, for the place where Jesus was crucified was near the city; and it was written in Hebrew, in Latin, and in Greek. The chief priests of the Jews then said to Pilate, "Do not write, 'The King of the Jews,' but, 'This man said, I am King of the Jews.'" Pilate answered, "What I have written I have written." When the soldiers had crucified Jesus they took his garments and made four parts, one for each soldier; also his tunic. But the tunic was without seam, woven from top to bottom; so they said to one another, "Let us not tear it, but cast lots for it to see whose it shall be." This was to fulfil the scripture, "They parted my garments among them, and for my clothing they cast lots."

Mat 27:39-43 - And those who passed by derided him, wagging their heads and saying, "You who would destroy the temple and build it in three days, save yourself! If you are the Son of God, come down from the cross." So also, the chief priests, with the scribes and elders, mocked him, saying, "He saved others; he cannot save himself. He is the King of Israel; let him come down now from the cross, and we will believe in him. He trusts in God; let God deliver him now, if he desires him; for he said, 'I am the Son of God.'"

Lu 23:39-41 - One of the criminals who were hanged railed at him, saying, "Are you not the Christ? Save yourself and us!" But the other rebuked him, saying, "Do you not fear God, since you are under the same sentence of condemnation? And we indeed justly; for we are receiving the due reward of our deeds; but this man has done nothing wrong."

Lu 23:34 - And Jesus said, "Father, forgive them; for they know not what they do." And they cast lots to divide his garments.

Jo 19:25-27 - So the soldiers did this. But standing by the cross of Jesus were his mother, and his mother's sister, Mary the wife of Clopas, and Mary Mag'dalene. When Jesus saw his mother, and the disciple whom he loved standing near, he said to his mother, "Woman, behold, your son!" Then he said to the disciple, "Behold, your mother!" And from that hour the disciple took her to his own home.

Mat 27:46-50 - And about the ninth hour Jesus cried with a loud voice, "Eli, Eli, la'ma sabach-tha'ni?" that is, "My God, my God, why hast thou forsaken me?" And some of the bystanders hearing it said, "This man is calling Eli'jah." And one of them at once ran and took a sponge, filled it with vinegar, and put it on a reed, and gave it to him to drink. But the others said, "Wait, let us see whether Eli'jah will come to save him." And Jesus cried again with a loud voice and yielded up his spirit.

Mat 27:55-56 - There were also many women there, looking on from afar, who had followed Jesus from Galilee, ministering to him; among whom were Mary Mag'dalene, and Mary the mother of James and Joseph, and the mother of the sons of Zeb'edee.

Jo 19:31-34 - Since it was the day of Preparation, in order to prevent the bodies from remaining on the cross on the sabbath (for that sabbath was a high day), the Jews asked Pilate that their legs might be broken, and that they might be taken away. So the soldiers came and broke the legs of the first, and of the other who had been crucified with him; but when they came to Jesus and saw that he was already dead, they did not break his legs. But one of the soldiers pierced his side with a spear, and at once there came out blood and water.

Jo 19:38-42 - After this Joseph of Arimathe'a, who was a disciple of Jesus, but secretly, for fear of the Jews, asked Pilate that he might take away the body of Jesus, and Pilate gave him leave. So, he came and took away his body. Nicode'mus also, who had at first come to him by night, came bringing a mixture of myrrh and aloes, about a hundred pounds' weight. They took the body of Jesus, and bound it in linen cloths with the spices, as is the burial custom of the Jews. Now in the place where he was crucified there was a garden, and in the garden a new tomb where no one had ever been laid. So, because of the Jewish day of Preparation, as the tomb was close at hand, they laid Jesus there.

Mat 27:60 - and laid it in his own new tomb, which he had hewn in the rock; and he rolled a great stone to the door of the tomb, and departed.

Original Jefferson book …Smithsonian:
https://americanhistory.si.edu/JeffersonBible/

…………………………………………………………………………......

GOD/DIVINTY?
Not mentioned much by Jefferson, but center of our beliefs.

What is your God? Male? Female? Male/Female? Plaster? Wood? Gold? A Spirit? A puff of smoke? As a Greek philosopher once said, "if a horse had a god, it would be a horse."

Ron's God is a state of consciousness that created all the laws found, and those to be found, in the laws of physics. Thus "God" can't break those laws of physics that this entity created. Ron's God is in his mind, in his emotions, in his actions. He believes that entities, Anointed/Messiah/Christos, like Jesus and others, certified their "divinity" by their actions and their teachings. Actions are much more powerful and have more profound, lasting effects than labels. Jesus/Y'shua is divine because of his actions and teachings and not by pronouncement. Ron sees "God" in a living tree. In fact, he has one tree in particular that he relates to as his "God" force. Yes, he prays for endurance with "God's" help to get through current and long-lasting problems. "God" is within Ron. Ron can see "God" in others by their actions and words they do and say. The "God" entity (The Force); Jesus, the human example and teacher; Spirit, the binding force, the personal connection.

Other opinions by other Practical Theologians

God is a Spirit, infinite, eternal, and unchangeable, in His being, wisdom, power, holiness, justice, goodness, and truth.

For me, God is the ultimate reality that encompasses and pervades all of creation. Or as is attributed to the apostle Paul in Acts 17, God is the reality in which we live and move and have our being. We are the fish to God's water; creation is dependent on the pervasive presence of God for its survival. Subsequently, God cannot divorce God's self from creation any more than the water can choose to remove itself from the fish. Every aspect of creation is infused with the Divine, beckoning us to recognize the ever-present reality of God that sustains all things.

God is one of the names which we give to that eternal, independent, and incomprehensible being, the creator of all things, who preserves and governs everything by his almighty power and wisdom, and who is the only object of our worship.

<u>Who is God?</u> God is the force of life and of love. God shows up in surprising ways, always larger and more clever than we can imagine. Humans try to put framework and descriptors on God, but they are never complete, thank goodness. Humans also try to play God, or ignore or supplant God, but through wars and oppression and all kinds of ego-driven pestilence the force of life keeps birthing creation, and the power of love continues to sustain hope and community and forgiveness and, thus, peace. God reigns.

<u>What is divinity?</u> Divinity is the genuine presence of God, free of all imitations and denials.

We do not base our argument for God's existence upon the unattainable assumption that consciousness is a mystical facility in the mind, independent of reason. Nor upon the quality untenable assumption that every pronouncement of consciousness is an infallible echoing of the voice of God. We base it upon the fact that there is a moral order in the universe, mirrored in the stern commands of consciousness to do what is right and to avoid what is wrong.

God is all that is and is spiritual in nature. The so-called "physical" universe, including us, is technically non-physical. We are all part of a single Godhead. A good analogy would be that God is the ocean and we are individual drops in that ocean. God experiences novelty and change, not through us, but "as" us. When we interact with each other, we are at the same time interacting with God. When we are loving ourselves and one another, we are loving God. God becomes "personal" and makes him/her/itself known to us through human beings, especially

Jesus, who are temporarily incarnate. The technical term for my belief system is "Idealistic Monism."

The world, we inhabit must of had an origin; that origin must have consisted in a cause; that cause must have been intelligent; that intelligence must have been supreme; and that supreme, which always was and is supreme we know by the name of God.

In monotheistic thought, God is conceived of as the supreme being, creator deity, and principal object of faith. God is usually conceived as being omniscient (all-knowing), omnipotent (all-powerful), omnipresent (all-present) and as having an eternal and necessary existence. These attributes are used either in way of analogy or are taken literally. God is most often held to be incorporeal (immaterial). Incorporeality and corporeality of God are related to conceptions of transcendence (being outside nature) and immanence (being in nature) of God, with positions of synthesis such as the "immanent transcendence".

Some religions describe God without reference to gender, while others or their translations use sex-specific terminology. Judaism, for example, attributes only a grammatical gender to God, using terms such as "Him" or "Father" for convenience.

God has been conceived as either personal or impersonal. In theism, God is the creator and sustainer of the universe, while in deism, God is the creator, but not the sustainer, of the universe. In pantheism, God is the universe itself. In atheism, there is an absence of belief in God. In agnosticism, the existence of God is deemed unknown or unknowable. God has also been conceived as the source of all moral obligation, and the "greatest conceivable existent". Many notable philosophers have developed arguments for and against the existence of God.

To escape from evil we must be made, as far as possible, like God; and this resembles consistence in the coming just, and holy, and wise. — Plato

"Christians" going back outside the tent.

The following is the start of the split-up of the "Christian" faith.

Having nothing to do with the teachings of Jesus of Nazareth, the Christo.

There were regional differences in the practice of worshiping the Messiah, Christo, or as we call it today, "Christianity" within the Orthodox Church. But there was continuity among the pageantry and Liturgies. Then in 1054.

The **East–West Schism**, also called the **Great Schism** and the **Schism of 1054**, was the break of communion between what are now the Roman Catholic Church and Eastern Orthodox Churches, which had lasted until the 11th century. The Schism was the culmination of theological and political differences between the Christian East and West which had developed over the preceding centuries. The Roman Orthodox Church became the Roman Catholic Church.

A succession of ecclesiastical differences and theological disputes between the Greek East and Latin West pre-dated the formal rupture that occurred in 1054. Prominent among these were the issues of the procession of the Holy Spirit, whether leavened or unleavened bread should be used in the Eucharist, the Bishop of Rome's claim to universal jurisdiction, and the place of the See of Constantinople in relation to the Pentarchy.

Does anyone think that Jesus cared at all about these earthly issues such as these?

In 1053, the first step was taken in the process which led to formal schism: the Greek churches in southern Italy were forced either to close or to conform to Latin practices. In retaliation, the Ecumenical Patriarch of Constantinople Michael I Cerularius ordered the closure of all Latin churches in Constantinople. In 1054, the papal legate sent by Leo IX travelled to Constantinople for purposes that included refusing to Cerularius the title of "Ecumenical Patriarch" and insisting that he recognize the Pope's claim to be the head of all the churches. **Do you think that Jesus cared?** The main purpose of the papal legation was to seek help from the Byzantine Emperor in view of the Norman conquest of southern Italy and to deal with recent attacks by Leo of Ohrid against the use of unleavened bread and other Western customs, attacks that had the support of Cerularius. Historian Axel Bayer says the legation was sent in response to two letters, one from the Emperor seeking assistance in arranging a common military campaign by the eastern and western empires against the Normans, and the other from Cerularius. On the refusal of Cerularius to accept the demand, the leader of the legation, Cardinal Humbert of Silva Candida, O.S.B., excommunicated him, and in return Cerularius excommunicated Humbert and the other legates. This was only the first act in a centuries-long process that eventually became a complete schism. **What did any of this have in spreading Jesus's wisdom?**

The validity of the Western legates' act is doubtful, since Pope Leo had died and Cerularius' excommunication applied only to the legates personally. Still, the Church split along doctrinal, theological, linguistic, political, and geographical lines, and the fundamental breach has never been healed, with each side sometimes accusing the other of having fallen into heresy and of having initiated the division. The Latin led Crusades, the Massacre of the Latins in 1182, the West's retaliation in the Sacking of Thessalonica in 1185, the capture and pillaging of Constantinople by the Fourth Crusade in 1204, and the imposition of Latin patriarchs made reconciliation more difficult. Establishing Latin hierarchies in the Crusader states meant that there were two rival claimants to each of the patriarchal sees of Antioch, Constantinople, and Jerusalem, making the existence of schism clear. **None of this was taught by Jesus of Nazareth the Christo.**

Portions from the online Wikipedia encyclopedia.

Has the time come for us to rethink our priorities with regard to our commitment to our God? To the teachings, or to the tapestry, pageantry, and magic of a "religion"?

Summation of "Christianity" Today

Richard Goyette does a good job of summing up the "Christianity" of today: ... Church goers, especially evangelicals, tend to gravitate toward charismatic personalities who speak with a strong sense of authority. The evangelical mega-churches appear to be thriving under this kind of leadership. People gravitate towards this leadership style for several reasons:

1. Most people are uncomfortable with "shades of gray" when it comes to religion, ethics and morality. They want their theology to be clearly and unambiguously "spelled out" for them in more or less black & white terms.

2. Most people tend towards intellectual laziness and/or lack of self-confidence when it comes to serious Bible study and theological investigation. Instead, they would rather put their trust in a strong leader who they feel is more qualified than they are.

3. Most people would naturally defer to traditional teachings and the status quo when faced with the possible "reinterpretation" the Scriptures in order to accommodate the needs of a changing and evolving society. The moral and ethical values of our society are changing, in some ways for the better, and our access to information is also increasing. Advances in science and biblical criticism have shed new light on the historical context of the Scriptures and the nature of God. But change comes slowly because of the natural resistance people have to change.

4. Most Christians have developed a strong emotional attachment to their traditional beliefs, forms of worship, and social attachments. Breaking those bonds can result in severe emotional distress.

....